Cherrie

First Hundred Years

ABOVE: Boscombe FC 1910/11, with the Hampshire League (West Division) Cup ...
(back, l to r) S Knight, S Blachford, W Horne, A Williams, P Giles, P Bennett, W
Clarkson, G Parsley, W Cassidy, H Jenkins, J Brown, W Marsh, C Richardson; (middle)
H T Franklin, C Marsh, G Smith, B Penton, W Hayward, W Tarrant, R Whiterow, E
Manns, G Hutchings; (front) C Franklin, J P New, J Small, P Taylor, F J Franklin. This pho-
tograph of the first team to play at Dean Court was salvaged from an old building,
hence the paint splatters.

Cherries

First Hundred Years
AFC Bournemouth 1899-1999

Kevin Nash

RED POST

FRONTIS: Ian Cox (left) and Matt Holland, two of the most popular players of the 1990s

Reprinted 2002

First Published in 1999 by Red Post Books

ISBN 1-901533-52-2
Designed and Produced for Red Post Books
by Crispin Goodall

Printed and bound in Great Britain by
The Cromwell Press Ltd

Red Post Books
81 Saxonhurst Road
Bournemouth
Dorset
BH10 6JF

(01202) 511517

Contents

Acknowledgements

dedicated to
Amy and Harry

Special thanks to Mick Cunningham who compiled the statistics and provided some of the pictures, particularly for the early chapters. Thanks also to John Trelevan and Leigh Edwards who compiled the club history and championship souvenir booklet in 1987 which provided much of the background material, along with Tony Pullein's 1959 book Up The Cherries, now sadly out of print.

Thanks to the Daily Echo, Bournemouth, especially editor Neal Butterworth, for permission to use their photographs and cuttings, and to chief librarian and Cherries devotee Scott Harrison, who was a big, big help to me. The Echo's chief photographer Duncan Lee also provided much assistance, which is most appreciated. I would like at this point to pay tribute to the Echo and freelance photographers who took the pictures which form such an important part of this book – they include the late Harry Ashley, John Beasley, Paul Collins, Richard Crease, John Gilbride, Andy Horsfield, Duncan Lee, Corin Messer and Andy Scaysbrook. These people often work in cold, wet and windy conditions and deserve our admiration. Thanks too to all the past and present players, managers, directors and supporters (including the Three Ronnies – Hands, Old and Turner) who shared their memories with me. And, if you've just bought this book, thanks to you as well.

BOURNEMOUTH AND BOSCOMBE F.C. 1937-8.   PHOTO STANFORD.

On this page and the next, a pictorial scrapbook of memories we couldn't fit into the book....

CHAPTER

1

Early Days

BELOW: First team, 1899/1900
(back, l to r) Keats, J Spicer,
J C Nutt, S Davis, E Francis,
S Draper; (middle) C Smith,
C Stephenson, A Emery, C Kerley,
J Hookey, E Richardson; (front)
C Coxen, T Kerley, H Hanham

APRIL 19, 1998, a chilly, intermittently sunny Sunday afternoon. The giant scoreboard spelled out 'Wembley welcomes the Cherries', and 34,000 AFC Bournemouth supporters in the near-63,000 crowd looked up with a mixture of delight, relief and disbelief. Just over a year before their club had seemed doomed, destined to become the first Football League side to fold in mid-season since Aldershot five years earlier. The players weren't being paid, the two major shareholders were locked in a bitter boardroom battle and the Inland Revenue was poised

with a winding-up order for unpaid tax. The bank, which held a debenture on the ground, called in receivers, who uncovered debts of almost £5 million. Rumours swept the town – the club was certain to go under, the bank would sell the land to a super-market chain or luxury housing developers. The hard-core fans crossed their fingers and waited for a 'white knight', a busi-nessman with money to burn. And waited. And waited. Showbusiness promoter and long-time supporter Mel Bush made a bid, which he would later claim had been accepted, but which the receivers said was insufficient to satisfy the bank. With time rapidly running out a group of supporters formed a trust fund and called a meeting at a theatre in the town. Long queues snaked down the road an hour before the start, more than 2,000 people crammed into the Winter Gardens and buckets were passed round to raise a fighting fund. Europe's first com-munity club was born that night. The ranks of diehard fans were swollen by a surge of long-lost sympathisers and new-found followers. Pensioners handed over their savings, children gave

BELOW AND OPPOSITE TOP: It took a while to get in to their stride but Boscombe, pictured in 1906/07 (below) and 1908/09, soon started collecting trophies

up their pocket money. Youngsters appeared on the streets wearing red-and-black striped shirts instead of Arsenal and Liverpool replica kits. The bank, the Football League, the receivers and the creditors saw just how much the people of the region wanted their club to survive. But the courts and the Inland Revenue weren't going to be swayed by sympathy. A survival deal was thrashed out with just minutes to spare. But Cherries did more than just survive. They emerged from the

BELOW: William Pickford threw his considerable weight at the FA behind his hometown club

MR. PICKFORD AND HIS PENNY FARTHING.

11

ashes with enough impetus to reach Wembley for the first time in their history. Another year on, and the club prepared to celebrate a centenary that looked as though it was destined never to arrive. This is the story of AFC Bournemouth's first 100 years . . .

*

Bournemouth's football club is almost as old as the town. Or rather one of Bournemouth's football clubs, Bournemouth FC, also known as the Poppies, formed in 1875. But this is the history of another, more famous, club. Now known as AFC Bournemouth and Boscombe Community Club, AFC Bournemouth for short, alphabetically at least the top club in England. Also known as the Cherries. (As this century, millennium even, draws to a close and another sport, rugby union, takes its first troubled steps towards professionalism, clubs are called Falcons, Tigers, Saracens and Wasps. Back then, in a more genteel age, we had Cherries and Poppies.) Until the late 19th century there was little inhabited land between the port of

BELOW: Feverish excitement greets the visit in 1913 of the Wanderers, famous as the first winners of the FA Cup

Poole and historic Christchurch. Then some seriously rich people saw the potential of this previously undeveloped area of gorse and heather. Wealthy families – the Tregonwells, Cooper Deans and Meyricks, whose names would live on through the next century and beyond in roads, parks and estates – built palatial homes by the sea. They generated jobs, as did the developing road and rail links and the burgeoning

tourist trade boosted by the increased wealth from the industrial revolution. The population soared from a few hundred in the 1840s to 60,000 at the turn of the century. (By the year 2000 the figure was approaching 160,000.)

Bournemouth was always a refined sort of place. It was where people went to stroll by the sea and breathe in the ozone and pine scent wafting up from the chines. It had little heavy industry and was never destined to become a football hotbed like the blue-collar towns further north. But there was a growing number of resettled manual workers building this rapidly-thriving resort – and a strong link with the national game in the shape of William Pickford, a founder member of the Football Association, who lived at Pokesdown and would pedal his penny-farthing the 100 miles or so to London for meetings.

The first major football teams in the town, apart from the Poppies, long since a fixture in the local non-league scene, were connected to the big utilities, the transport, water, electricity and gas companies. But AFC Bournemouth had much more humble origins and emerged from the disbandment of Boscombe St John's Lads' Institute. Boscombe FC was formed in 1899 by a dozen people who met at a house in Gladstone Road, somewhere near the present-day Sovereign Centre shopping complex. Officers were elected at the Colonnade restaurant. Training was frowned upon and selection meetings took place under street lamps in Pokesdown to save on the cost of hiring com-

BELOW: Smile, please! This derby match in April 1914 between Boscombe and Bournemouth, Cherries v Poppies, was obviously a tense affair if the crowd's expressions are any guide

mittee rooms. The first captain was Charlie Hembery (also spelled Hemery and Emery in reports of the time) and his team-mates had names like 'Jumbo' Hookey, 'Pedlar' Palmer and 'Bimbo' Boys. The first match, against Christchurch Royal Artillery, took place on October 7 1899, 'before a fair number of spectators', reported the Christchurch Times. It was goalless at half-time, but the Artillery's superior physique and fitness told and they scored two goals in quick succession. 'Boscombe, however, played very pluckily and had hard lines in not scoring, once in particular from a shot by Tuck.' Charlie Stevenson did score a consolation but the first competitive game, in the Bournemouth and District Junior League, ended in defeat. It cost £5 10s a season to hire the pitch at Castlemain Road before the club moved to Kings Park in 1902. Boscombe won nothing until 1905-6 when they lifted the Hampshire Junior Cup. But from then until they were accepted into the Football League in 1923 they couldn't stop winning trophies, at least one a season. The start of this successful run coincided with the appointment of P W T 'Wilf' Hayward as club secretary, an association with a family of builders that has continued with a break of only a few months until the present day. Hayward stayed with the club until his death in 1941, when he was succeeded as a director by his son Reg. Reg's son Peter also became chairman and had a sponsors' lounge named after him and Peter's cousin Geoffrey was a director and life-president at the time of his death in 1999.

ABOVE: Boscombe FC, winners of the Page Croft Cup in 1920

Back in 1910 the club was beginning to build a reputation in the town and prominent local landowner J E Cooper-Dean JP granted a long lease on a piece of waste ground near Kings Park. Supporters levelled the earth and laid the turf. Hayward put up a stand to hold 300 spectators and a surrounding fence. The facility was hired out to cricket and tennis clubs to recoup some of the outlay. Players, including even star men 'Sergeant' Marsh and George Kitchen, apparently a very fine goalkeeper, had to change at the Portman Hotel about half-a-mile away and spectators paid 3d to get in – receipts for the first match at the new stadium at the start of the 1910/11 season totalled £65.

The club's first professional, Baven Penton, signed from Southampton for £10 the following season and picked up the grand total of 30s a week. The first season tickets were issued for the 1912/13 season – they cost 10s 6d in the grandstand and 5s for the rest of the ground. Boscombe's first appearance in the FA Cup came in 1913/14 and the First World War brought an abrupt end to their one and only season in the South-Eastern League. The team had struggled at this higher standard. Boscombe played Southampton Reserves in January 1915.

ABOVE: Now that's what you call a line-up ... with Kings Park pavilion looming out of the mist

This much is known because there is a postcard showing soldiers, billeted in the area for training, watching the game. But there is no record of the result or any other games being played during that terrible period. People had other, much more important things on their mind. A whole generation of young men had been decimated in the trenches. No one kept score in the famous Christmas Day kick-about between German and British troops ... but it was probably the most poignant match of all time.

After the war had ended the club returned to the Hampshire League. There was strong support nationally for the formation of a Third Division of the Football League, and this came about in 1920. The resulting reshuffle saw Boscombe move up to the Southern League. They reached the FA Cup fifth qualifying round in 1921/22 and the following season drew at Third Division Exeter City before going out in a replay. The Cherry Stripes (as they were known because of their distinctive red-and-white kit) were now a non-league force to be reckoned with.

The Big League

Wilf Hayward lobbied the First and Second Division clubs for support and Boscombe were elected to the Football League at the first time of asking in 1923. William Pickford's backing was also crucial. A new era had dawned and the directors decided it was time for a change of name – the club became Bournemouth and Boscombe Athletic FC (although even today many supporters, especially the older ones, still refer to the team as Boscombe and the chant 'Boscombe, Back Of The Net' tumbles down from the terraces.) Scotsman Harry Kinghorn was the first trainer. Most of the players lived in digs close to the ground and spectators either walked, cycled or took the train to Boscombe station and strolled the rest of the way across Kings Park. Fans entered the Penny on the Ball competition and the matchball was the prize. The first League game ended in a 3-1 defeat at Swindon in front of almost 10,000 spectators. Boscombe played in unfamiliar blue jerseys because of a colour clash with the Robins. What was to have been the first home match four days later was washed out, but the return against Swindon eventually went ahead the following Saturday and finished goalless. Fans of the fledgling club soon became used to this sort of stale fare. Boscombe failed to score in 10 of their 21 home games that season, winning just six at Dean Court. The first League win was at Exeter, 2-0, and the first home victory against the same opposition a week later.

A giant goalkeeper called Carr, just a tad under 6ft 9ins, starred in a friendly against FA Cup holders Bolton in that first season – for once a 0-0 score reflected an heroic performance. That was a rare high spot in an otherwise undistinguished

ABOVE: Scotsman Harry Kinghorn was a tower of strength in the club's early days

RIGHT: Bournemouth & Boscombe in the early 1920s (back, l to r) Butt, Saxon, Wilson, Lamb, Leitch, Richardson; (front) Buchanan, Readman, Smith, Miles, McCulloch

BELOW: Wilf Hayward, an early driving force whose family would play a big part at Boscombe over the forthcoming century

Division Three (South) campaign. Boscombe finished second from bottom, only QPR fared worse, but both clubs were re-elected. Hard man W 'Dossie' Miles signed from Bournemouth Tramways and made an immediate impact the following season but the club was hit by the first of many financial crises and looked doomed to fold by Christmas. They weren't helped by an ignominious FA Cup defeat at non-league Yeovil, giant-killers even then, but salvation arrived in the form of the sort of man the fans had been crying out for – prodigious centre-forward Ronnie Eyre, who signed from Sheffield Wednesday in 1924 and went on to score more than 250 goals over the next nine years. Leslie Knighton, ex-Arsenal, took over managerial duties from Kinghorn and Boscombe reached the dizzy heights of eighth place in 1925/6, when they also surged to the fourth round of the FA Cup where they pulled out a plum home tie with Bolton, who fielded seven of the 1923 side which had become the first to lift the trophy at Wembley. It was a very wet day and the attendance of 10,165 fell below the 11,950 who saw the game against Reading in the previous round. The slightly disappointing turn-out may also have had something to do with the fact that ticket prices were doubled. Cherries were five minutes from a famous victory when England international David Jack snatched a 2-2 draw for Wanderers who comfortably won the replay as a springboard to another appearance in the final. (They also signed Boscombe forward Leslie Roberts for £2,000, a tidy sum in those days, straight after the match at Burnden Park). The following season was notable for another good Cup run. A record 13,409 watched the third round tie against Liverpool, including some in a temporary stand usual-

17

ly erected at agricultural shows. A late goal, with more than a suspicion of offside about it, earned a Liverpool side boasting six internationals an Anfield replay which they won 4-1. But already Boscombe were earning a reputation as a tough nut to crack for star-studded visiting teams. The Cherries Supporters Club became (with Brentford, Brighton, Northampton,

ABOVE: Mr C E Sutcliffe, League vice-president, opens the new stand on August 27 1927

Charlton, and Plymouth) one of the six founder members of the National Federation of Football Supporters Clubs in 1927. The town was behind the team, now making a profit, and a £10,000 ground improvement scheme was drawn up. Wilf Hayward supervised the purchase and re-construction of a grandstand formerly used at the British Empire Exhibition at Wembley in 1925. It was 360ft long, held 3,700 spectators and included a boardroom, dressing-rooms and offices. The new stand gave Dean Court a majestic appearance and the team produced a fitting 2-0 win over Swindon following the official opening at the start of the 1927/28 season.

Cherries lost only three home games in the League, but struggled away. For the first time they were drawn away to First Division opposition in the FA Cup, losing at Sheffield Wednesday. Eyre finished the season with 30 goals and Knighton was lured back to a higher standard of football, at Birmingham, whom he led to the FA Cup final in 1931. Frank Richards took over as manager and Boscombe enjoyed their best pre-war season in 1928/29, reaching the fifth round of the FA Cup, where they lost in a replay at West Ham, thus missing out on the mouthwatering prospect of a local derby at Fratton Park, Portsmouth. The first round draw had paired Boscombe with non-league Poole Town, just a few miles down the road. It was the first (and remains the only) time the two teams met in a national competition. A disappointing 6,000 people (Poole had expected double that) watched the game at Fernside Road,

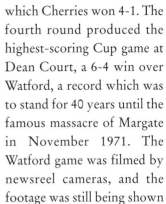

which Cherries won 4-1. The fourth round produced the highest-scoring Cup game at Dean Court, a 6-4 win over Watford, a record which was to stand for 40 years until the famous massacre of Margate in November 1971. The Watford game was filmed by newsreel cameras, and the footage was still being shown

ABOVE: The balding Ronnie Eyre holds centre stage in the front row of this team photo, and dominated the 1930s

in local cinemas 20 years later. The Western world was plunged into depression in the early 1930s. So, less seriously, were Cherries. They were forced to apply for re-election for the second time in 1933/34, attendances fell and the directors dug deep into their own pockets to prop up the ailing club.

MEMORIES – Sid Kerley, 80, was living in Gloucester Road, within a few hundred yards of Dean Court, in 1999. He started watching Cherries 70 years earlier, in 1929 . . .

'My uncles, Charlie and Ted, played for the club when they turned professional before World War I. Ronnie Eyre was the top man, Jack Hayward the best defender. Jimmy Blair was another great player. We would get between 3,000 and 4,000 just for reserve games, amazing. I lived in Winton then and used to cycle to games. You'd leave your bike outside and it would still be there at the end of the game, not like these days. When World War II broke out I was called up with three of the players – Tommy Paton, Jack Kirkham and Fred Wilson. I was with Wilson all the way through, six years in France, Belgium, Holland and Germany. Fred was very regimental, same as on the pitch. He finished up a captain in the Army, I remained a private. After the war Harry Kinghorn asked me to sign for the club but the gas and water company had kept my old job open and I was 26 then. Harry was a bloody good bloke, he did everything for the club.'

CHAPTER
3

War Stops Play

Boscombe, renowned Cup fighters, even struggled in the sudden-death games, losing their unbeaten FA Cup home record to Fulham. They also suffered a 7-0 stuffing in the League at Torquay, who had not previously won in three months. In February 1930 Sammy Beswick became the first Boscombe player to earn an international call-up, for the England Amateur XI. The next season saw the first international match at Dean Court, England Amateurs beating Wales 5-0 in front of 9,000 spectators. Harry Kinghorn was England's trainer that day, meaning he had to miss the club's match at Norwich and bringing to an end his proud record of having attended every first team away game since election to the League.

Frank Richards resigned as manager in October 1930 and was replaced by Billy Birrell, one of more than 100 applicants. Birrell, formerly with Middlesbrough and Raith Rovers, lost his first game in charge and things didn't get much better, although Cherries did make the fourth round of the FA Cup in 1932, where they were hammered 7-0 by Sheffield Wednesday. Attendances slumped and the players didn't get paid that summer. The board launched a Shilling Fund appeal through the local press – it would not be the last time the begging bowl was brought out. Players were sold to raise funds, including Reg Trim, who went on to star under Herbert Chapman at Arsenal. Ronnie Eyre retired after a glorious career. He never owned a car and enjoyed fishing on the River Stour near his Iford home. He went on to play football for Christchurch and Bournemouth Electric, where he also starred on the cricket pitch, always with a cap covering his bald head. It proved hard to replace stars

ABOVE: Billy Birrell in his younger days as a player

BELOW: Bert Bliss, ex-Spurs

RIGHT: Bournemouth and
Boscombe 1934/35
(back, l to r) Moralee, Parker,
Richardson, Messer, Pincott,
Randall, Richardson, Parris;
(middle) White, Gold, Fletcher,
Mortimer, Chalmers, Mellors,
Richmond, Moore; (front) Turner,
Ritchie, Farrow, Tait, Cameron,
Twiss, Smith

like Eyre, Jack Hayward and Jack Whitehouse. Desperate times
called for desperate measures. A share issue raised £4,000 for new
players. But season 1933/34 was the worst the club has ever experienced on the field, with 100 goals conceded, and it ended in
another plea for re-election. Thankfully, it was almost a fore-
gone conclusion – Boscombe and bottom club Cardiff received
48 votes each. Hopeful applicants Folkestone got none.

Things couldn't get much worse. Again the people of the
town came to the rescue, answering an appeal for increased
support by buying season tickets in record numbers for 1934/35.
All this after the worst season in the club's relatively brief history. New signings included ex-Spurs centre-half Alf Messer as
player-coach and Eddie Parris, a left-winger from Bradford
Park Avenue, described in those pre-politically-correct times
as the club's first 'coloured' player. Cherries finished 17th, no
great shakes, but at least avoided the ignominy of again seeking re-election. Coventry became the first visiting team to score
five at Dean Court. Birrell left for QPR and the first really big-
name manager arrived at Bournemouth – Bob Crompton, ex-
Blackburn full-back, whose record for the most England caps,
42, was eventually broken by Wolves' Billy Wright. With the
change of manager came a change of strip, red and white striped
shirts were replaced by red with white collars. How times have
changed. It took a dozen years for Cherries to make their first
fashion statement. Nowadays some clubs change their kit more
often than supermodels. 'Owd Bob' Crompton started well –
1935/6 was the best for nine years, with a final placing of eighth

BELOW: 'Owd Bob' Crompton,
in and out in the flash of a 'tache

BOSCOMBE BID FOR FOR PROMOTION
(Evening Echo 19th September, 1936)

– but left as suddenly as he had arrived, in August 1936. Charles Bell, his replacement, had coaching experience in several countries including Italy, France, Portugal and Brazil. He joined from a somewhat less exotic location – Mansfield. Bell was a firm believer in developing young players, and set up an A team, which was based in New Milton and played in the Hampshire League. The newly-opened South Stand increased the covered accommodation to 13,000. Once again Swindon were the visitors on the date of the official opening, as they had been when the Main Stand was inaugurated, and once again Swindon lost, this time 5-2. A good season followed. Boscombe finished sixth, their best position until the onset of World War II. In the Cup they faced Everton, including 'Dixie' Dean, Cliff Britton, Ted Sagar and Joe Mercer, at Goodison Park and went down 5-0. Some consolation was the £2,200 windfall from a 35,000 gate.

ABOVE: Bert Thain, came to Cherries from Chelsea in 1931

LEFT: A cartoon of Charles Bell's side from the Evening Echo, September 1936

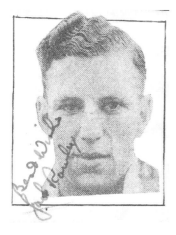

ABOVE: Jack Rowley went on to play for England and Man Utd

ABOVE: Bill Voisey moved down from London in the mid-1920s

Cherries made it into Europe for the first time in 1937/38, visiting Rotterdam to play the Dutch national side who wanted a warm-up for an international against France. Bell made the most of his contacts to strengthen the team. During World War I he had served under Major Frank Buckley, the famous Wolves manager - and he took several players deemed surplus to requirements by his old Army boss including defenders Fred Marsden, Bill Smith and Freddie Pincott (whose skill at shutting out centre-forwards was matched only by his amazing appetite for milkshakes, according to Inside Football magazine), forwards Bill Langley and Freddie Shaw, and wingers Bob Redfern and Jack Rowley (who joined Manchester United after just a few months at Dean Court and went on to score six goals in six England appearances.) Bell would oversee full-scale practice matches every Tuesday morning – first team forwards against reserve defenders and vice-versa – from a seat in the Main Stand, bellowing instructions over the public address system. His occasionally industrial language prompted the odd complaint from residents in nearby Thistlebarrow Road. At one stage that season Bournemouth were up among the leaders but tailed off to finish 13th.

The following campaign, the last to be completed before the outbreak of the war, was even more mediocre, with Boscombe finishing 15th. Goalkeeper Len Brooks did a vanishing act after training one day in September 1938. He later turned up in Bristol, claimed to be worried about his health and said he was retiring from the game. He promptly signed for Colchester. Custodians have always tended to be an eccentric breed but Brooks wasn't greatly missed because in March 1939 his replacement, Ken Bird, linked for the first time with right-back Marsden, left-back Joe Sanaghan and centre-half Wilson – these four would all return to become stout defensive stalwarts after the war ended. Bell, three years at the club, had put together a side of real potential and his youth policy was beginning to bear fruit when he was forced to step down because of ill health. He would sit on the balcony of his house in Kings Park and greet the players on their way to the ground before his death in June, and the following month long-serving Harry Kinghorn was promoted from caretaker-manager. On September 2 1939

Boscombe thrashed Northampton 10-0 at Dean Court, with Jack Kirkham scoring a hat-trick. But the players and fans were tense. They had more important things than football on their minds. War broke out the following day and the result was wiped from the record books as the season drew to a premature close after just three competitive games.

Boscombe continued to put out a team in the Southern Regional League and the FA Cup for a couple of seasons. Friendlies were arranged against such teams as Southampton, Torquay and West Ham, and Boscombe fielded guest players including Matt Busby (who was stationed at Aldershot and made his last appearance as a player in an 8-1 win against Bristol City in a war victory celebration match on September 22 1945) and legendary Charlton goalkeeper Sam Bartram, billeted at the Royal Bath Hotel. Dean Court became a tem-

ABOVE: Harry Gilmore joined Bournemouth from Hull

LEFT: Bournemouth & Boscombe pictured in 1937/38

BELOW: Cigarette card

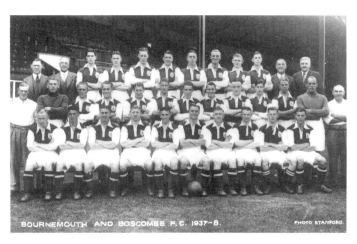

porary home for 500 French soldiers following the escape from Dunkirk in 1940. They slept in or under the Main Stand and received gifts of food and clothing from local people. British troops also stayed there later in the war and the ground was used for inter-Services matches and also hosted a baseball game organised by American soldiers based in the Purbecks. Kinghorn lovingly cared for the playing surface and even re-laid part of it by using a wheelbarrow to shift turf from a quarter-of-a-mile away. He also kept in touch with as many of the players as possible, including Marsden (who guested for Aldershot), Sanaghan (Belfast Distillery) and Wilson, who all

BOURNEMOUTH & BOS.

ABOVE: Troops and helpers at
Dean Court during World War II

ABOVE: Bob Redfern, pictured in
1999, joined from Wolves

visited when on home leave. Kinghorn said, 'Their first words were, "Let's have a look at the pitch".'

MEMORIES – Bob Redfern, aged 81 when we spoke at his Northbourne home in 1999, was a schoolteacher in Bournemouth after retiring from professional football . . .

'I remember vividly the Northampton game the day before war broke out. I was walking to the ground with Freddie Smith and a few of the other lads and we were all talking about how hot it was. The pitch was bone-hard but as were getting changed there was a cloudburst and we could hear the rain pelting down. It was over in minutes and the sun was back out when we kicked off, but the surface was perfect. I had a dream game, scored twice, made seven and got brought down for Fred Marsden's penalty. We were due to play at Cardiff a couple of days later but we all listened to the Prime Minister on the wireless at the ground on the Sunday and we knew we wouldn't be playing again for a while. Myself, Joe Riley and Jack Rowley were known as the three Rs. Charlie Bell was a players' manager and a good coach. We would play the ball in triangles around the opposition. That was a good team. If things had been different we could have gone places together.'

Success at Last

Wilf Hayward, the driving force through the early stages of the club's history, died in 1941. His son Reg joined the board. Some players never returned from the battlefield (Boscombe lost inside-left Peter Monaghan, killed in Holland, and left-half Wally Chalmers) while others missed the best years of their sporting careers. Jack Kirkham, signed from Wolves in 1938 and with an impressive 26 goals in 47 appearances, was taken prisoner but escaped from Italy and returned home via Switzerland to lead the Royal Hampshires on parade through Bournemouth. Secretary Tommy Locks, a volunteer in the Service Corps, was captured during the Greek Campaign in April 1941 and organised a camp football team which was allowed to play sides from other camps in the area.

LEFT: Back from the war . . . and big crowds packed in to Dean Court to celebrate

ABOVE: Towelling down ... (back, left to right) Joe Sanaghan, Ernie Tagg, Fred Marsden; (centre) Ken Bird; (front) Jack Percival, Jack McDonald

Boscombe only had one player, Tommy Paton (like Kirkham, an ex-Hampshire Regiment man), in full-time training when the game picked up again in 1945 although they had first call on those players who were registered before 1939. The Football League arranged a transitional season, organised on a regional basis, as life returned to something approaching normality. This was the year when Cherries won their first major trophy, the League Three (South) Cup. In the semi-final replay at Shepherds Bush they beat QPR 1-0 in a match lasting 136 minutes. At the end of three periods of extra-time the game was still goalless and it was agreed that the first team to score would go through. Kirkham finally found the back of the net in the first minute of the fourth additional period – who said 'golden goals' were a recent innovation? Boscombe faced Walsall in the final in front of almost 20,000 spectators at Stamford Bridge. Again a single goal settled it, scored by Jack McDonald in the ninth minute.

Bird, Marsden, Sanaghan and Wilson were ever-present throughout the 1946/47 season, which ended with the club in seventh place and a goal ratio of 72 for and 54 against, easily the best in their League history to that point. As shown before and since, goals bring in the crowds. A record 18,438 watched the FA Cup third round tie against Derby at Dean Court. The legendary Raich Carter got the second in a comfortable 2-0 win for the visitors. At the end of the season the stalwart Kinghorn retired to his native Scotland, where he passed away in 1955. His replacement was another Scot, Harry Lowe, who joined from

RIGHT: League Division Three (South) Cup winners 1945/46 ... (back, left to right) Dai Woodward, Fred Rowell, Fred Wilson, Ken Bird, Joe Sanaghan, Paddy Gallacher; (front) Tommy Paton, Jack Kirkham, Fred Marsden, Ernie Tagg Jack McDonald

Southern League Guildford City. Lowe was soon on a high, steering the club to second place after a seven-game unbeaten start to the 1947/48 season. The manager, speaking at a Round Table dinner, described the players he had inherited as, 'a grand set of fellows.' But a drop in form prompted Lowe to sign a man whose name still inspires awe among older supporters. Jimmy Blair, a hugely-gifted Scottish international playmaker, signed from Blackpool for a record £5,000, a huge

BELOW: Boscombe 1948-49

sum for such a small club but still a bargain, replacing Paton who joined Watford to sever a strong link with the pre-war team. Blair, a real character and a committed Socialist, distributed copies of the Daily Worker in the dressing-room and worked on a farm near Hurn. When he went to away matches he would cycle to Pokesdown train station and leave his bike under a hedge for the ride home upon his return. Blair also soon put a stop to Lowe's attempts to instigate team talks. At an inquest into a defeat, when the manager asked where things had gone wrong, he said to the manager, 'You're the problem.' But he pulled the strings to put Cherries back on course in the League and they also reached the third round of the FA Cup where they entertained mighty Wolves at Dean Court. Almost 24,000 people crammed in to the ground on a sunny January day in 1948. The Midlands giants included Billy Wright, Bert Williams and Jimmy Mullen. The normally reliable Bird flapped at a Mullen cross and punched the ball into his own net. Mullen soon added a second and South African Dudley Milligan's goal was no more than a consolation. (Milligan, who used to pretend to comb his curly hair on the pitch and joked about his attraction to the ladies, was described as 'mad as a hatter and hard as nails' by admiring teammates.) By April Cherries were locked in a promotion battle with QPR. The two teams met in a crucial game at Bournemouth with 25,700 inside the ground and 6,000 locked

ABOVE: Big keeper Ken Bird
BELOW: Brilliant Jimmy Blair

ABOVE: Who's a pretty boy then? Dudley Milligan, nail-hard mad hatter according to teammates

RIGHT: Arriving in Manchester for the big game against United

BELOW: Secretary Tommy Locks commentates on the QPR game to the 6,000 locked-out fans

outside listening to a commentary by the secretary Tommy Locks. The game was a let-down with the visitors edging a dour affair 1-0. Rangers went on to clinch the title but Boscombe, who finished four points adrift as runners-up, set no fewer than nine new club records including 24 wins, 11

away, and just 35 goals conceded. Unfortunately, only one team went up – and that was QPR.

A new-look line-up for 1948/49 included Doug McGibbon, who scored 30 goals in 31 games and would surely have beaten Ronnie Eyre's record had he signed from Fulham earlier than late September. League success the previous season earned exemption from the FA Cup until round three when Cherries travelled to play Manchester United at Maine Road (Old Trafford had been destroyed by German bombers and was being rebuilt) before a crowd of 55,000. United fielded nine of the team who had won the Cup the previous season and totally outclassed Boscombe, winning 6-0. But third place in the League represented a pleasing level of consistency. Bird and right-back Laurie Cunningham, who joined from Barnsley to replace the long-serving Marsden, were ever-present. This was also the season when one of Bournemouth's most popular characters joined the club. Tony Pullein's book 'Up The Cherries', published to mark the 50th anniversary, described Arnold Stephens as, 'one of Boscombe's tiniest players with one of the biggest hearts.' He arrived from Queen of the South in December and played 17 games that season, scoring five times. He was quick, comfortable on either wing and 'his unfettered energy made him almost impossible to keep under control.' He made 36 appearances the following season, with four goals, but was struck down by a severe unspecified illness in the summer of 1950. He was bed-bound for many months and specialists told him he would never play again. 'Steve' recovered sufficiently to take a job with the Southern Electricity Board and became trainer-coach for the company team. He poured all his energy in to regaining full fitness and ran countless miles along the beach. In 1953 he persuaded Cherries to give him another chance and within a few weeks was back in the first team. But the following season the sparkle was gone and he was relegated to the reserves. In April 1955 he had a kidney removed. The following month he died, aged just 27. Pullein said he was, 'a great sportsman who paid the supreme price for the game he loved.' The Golden Jubilee season of 1949/50 kicked off with a home defeat in front of a big crowd against relegated Nottingham Forest. There was a celebration banquet at the Pavilion Theatre with FA secretary Sir Stanley Rous among the guests and Cream of Boscombe Soup, Gateaux Dean Court and Bavarois aux Cherries on the menu. Blair, who had made 80 League appearances and created many of the goals for Milligan and McGibbon, moved to Orient. Bird's benefit match, on his 200th appearance, drew the biggest crowd of the season, 20,385, for the game against Notts County whose awesome centre-forward Tommy Lawton was shut out in a 3-0 win.

For the first time Boscombe beat a team from a higher division in the FA Cup, Jack Cross's goal at Bradford Park Avenue lining up the prospect of a first competitive meeting with Southampton in the fourth round. Northampton hadn't read the script, however, and beat both Saints and Cherries, after a replay. Life was never easy for football managers. Lowe had done pretty well but he was sacked and replaced by Jack Bruton in March 1950. Bruton was a non-smoking teetotaller – the players wouldn't even talk about going for a pint in his hearing. Poor away form blighted any hopes of promotion in the early 1950s when Nancy, from France, and Hamborn 07, from Germany,

BELOW: Jack Cross scored 64 goals in 137 League games between 1947/53

ABOVE: Laurie Cunningham

visited Boscombe as part of the Festival of Britain celebrations. The Football League raised the minimum admission charge for 1951/52 to 1s 9d and disappointing gates at Dean Court showed supporters felt they weren't getting value for money. Cherries were infuriatingly inconsistent. Bird retired from professional football and joined Dorchester. The reliable Cunningham struggled through illness (he contracted pleurisy which kept him out for nine months) and injury. At the end of 1951 Bruton

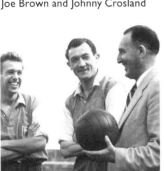

BELOW: Jack Bruton (right) with Joe Brown and Johnny Crosland

RIGHT: Tommy Godwin, a character and a great goalkeeper

broke the club's transfer record to sign Les Eyre for £6,000 from Norwich. The following summer he made one of the club's best ever signings – Tommy Godwin (whose Eire recall in 1956 made him the first full international to play for Boscombe) joined from Leicester and became hugely popular with the fans and fellow-players over the next 10 years. Chelsea centre-half Harry Hughes, who would go on to skipper the 1957 side which brought national prominence to the town, signed on the same day as Godwin. Bruton also spotted the potential of Peter Harrison, a slight but swift winger from Leeds, and previously-unknown striker Stan Newsham. Season 1953/54 was notable for the first competitive meeting between Bournemouth and Southampton. In fact it was like waiting ages for a bus then being faced by a fleet, with four games between the clubs in a few months. The first encounter came in the first round of the FA Cup. Boscombe, in their 'unlucky' green and white change strip, were fortunate to scrape a last-minute equaliser at The Dell but won the replay 3-1. The score-

line was the same in the League match at Dean Court but Saints took their revenge 2-1 at home.

In 1955 Cherries reached the FA Cup third round for the first time in five years, drawing holders West Bromwich Albion at home. Captain Johnny Crosland became the first Boscombe player to appear on TV with a live interview on BBC's Sportsview being watched by an estimated 13 million viewers. Ticket prices were bumped up, attracting heavy criticism from supporters, with many of them boycotting the match, and 'only' 23,000 turned up

although the gate receipts of just over £4,100 were easily a record. Albion fielded eight of their Wembley team and won 1-0. Godwin was recalled by the Republic of Ireland while local

ABOVE: Captain Crosland became the first Boscombe player to appear on live TV

LEFT: Line-up for 1955-56 ...
(back, left to right) Joe O'Boyle,
Laurie Cunningham, Albert
Keetley, Tommy Godwin, Bill
Heath, Dennis Hall, Ian
Drummond, Dai Woodward;
(middle) Joe Clare, Brian Siddall,
Joe Brown, Eric Sanderson,
Harry Hughes, Peter Rushworth,
Ken Whiteside, Malcolm
Macdonald, Arthur Cunliffe,
Harry Stace; (front) Nelson Stiffle,
Eddie McManus, Derek Leaver,
Ollie Norris, Jack Bruton, Johnny
Crosland, Eric Wilkinson,
Stan Newsham, Ian Allen,
Peter Harrison

discovery Roy Littlejohn starred for England Amateurs and was
selected for the Great Britain Olympic side. The post-war boom
had petered out by 1955 and another rise in the minimum admission charge, to 2s did not help struggling clubs like Boscombe.
Support dropped off alarmingly. Chairman Reg Hayward said
the club had lost almost £6,000 the previous year and that unless
the public rallied round players would have to be sold. Bruton, who
made some exceptional signings during his six years at
Bournemouth, was sacked. He accepted his dismissal as 'all
part of the game', and wished his successor luck. He would
soon return as chief scout. Hayward explained that 'a change
of manager would be beneficial to the club.' Even he probably
didn't expect to be proved so right, so quickly.

ABOVE: Laurie Cunningham at
home in Charminster in 1999

MEMORIES - Laurie Cunningham, an RAF fighter pilot during World
War II, played over 300 games at right-back under three different managers (Lowe, Bruton and Cox) before retiring to run a newsagents in
Bennett Road, Charminster ...
'Reg Hayward fixed my family up with a flat in Orcheston Road which
was a big factor in me choosing Bournemouth because Coventry were
also interested and I played off one club against the other. Jack Bruton
was a real gentleman and he left it up to the trainer Arthur Cunliffe to
prepare us for games. There were very few team talks or tactics. The
wage when I retired in 1958 was £14, quite a lot considering the
national average was about £4 10s. I started the newsagents soon after
I arrived at the club and I would get up at 5.30am to do the deliveries
before cycling over to the ground for training. It was a happy place and
there were some great characters – Dai Woodward, Blair, Godwin and
Crosland, who we'd call 'King John.' Freddie Cox used to get us in for
extra training in the afternoons and he would vary the tactics. In those
days the ball used to get really heavy and full-backs like myself would
give opposing wingers a whack early in the game. If they came back for
more you knew you were in for a tough afternoon.'

Giant Killers

Sam Bartram was briefly linked with the manager's job but it went to Freddie Cox, the assistant at West Brom and a former Arsenal player. Season ticket prices were reduced to combat falling crowds. The home average for the previous season had been 8,000, down from 9,600 the previous year and 4,000 short of the break-even figure. But Cox and his players sent attendances through the roof with some sparkling football. Although new to senior management Cox was an instant success. Some of his ideas were years ahead of their time. He introduced a 'deep-lying' centre-forward (a role that would be deployed to great effect many years later by players like Dennis Bergkamp and Eric Cantona) and favoured all-out attack. He also tried to outwit the opposition by putting the players in unfamiliar shirt numbers – Tony Pullein claimed in his book that 'this proved to be a match-winning tactic on more than one occasion.' Were 1950s footballers and their managers really that gullible? Cox improved fitness levels and increased competition for places. If the more experienced players didn't fit in with his plans – which included hurdling, skipping and sprint training – he was quick to replace them with youngsters who did.

Boscombe were never content with one or two goals and the fans loved it. Shrewsbury were hit for six, Swindon for seven and Cherries won 4-0 at Reading: all within three months of the new boss taking over. But the big man's first season will be forever remembered for an astonishing run in the FA Cup. Burton Albion of the Birmingham Senior League were demolished 8-0 in front of 13,000-plus fans at Dean Court in the first round with Ollie Norris getting a hat-trick and Stan Newsham

ABOVE: Good morning, this is Freddie Cox calling

RIGHT: Reg Cutler's goal knocked out mighty Wolves at Molineux

BELOW: Nelson Stiffle scored a superb solo goal against Spurs

BELOW RIGHT: Ollie Norris (white shirt) makes a nuisance of himself with this determined challenge against Manchester United goalkeeper Ray Wood

two. It was the first step on what would turn out to be a glorious and so far unique journey to the sixth round. Cherries started with a big psychological advantage in round two. Swindon, although drawn at home, were understandably wary following their pounding in the League. A single goal by Reg Cutler, Cox's first signing, settled it. Accrington Stanley, from the Third Division Northern Section, visited Bournemouth in round three. A colour clash saw the home team emerge in blue and white shirts borrowed from Portsmouth, 2-0 the score. Then it was away to Wolves, third in the First Division. They

still had Williams, Wright and Mullen from the side which had beaten Boscombe in 1948. They also had Ron Flowers and Peter Broadbent. It looked like curtains. Four thousand fans travelled up to Molineux from the south coast. After just five minutes Newsham squared the ball across goal, Williams dived and missed only for Eddie Stuart to hack clear. The onrushing Cutler arrived a split-second later and crashed into an upright, fell into the goal and caught his studs on the net, bringing the frame crashing down and causing a seven-minute hold-up. The repair job must have been pretty good because the goal was still standing after Nelson Stiffle had crashed a shot against the bar. The First Division side must have thought they were off the hook but then Cutler put the ball, rather than himself, in the net five minutes before the interval. Harry Hughes played most of the second half with concussion and Norris was struggling with a groin strain as Wolves piled on the pressure. But defender Arnold Woollard snuffed out the threat of £25,000 Harry Hooper, Mullen had a goal ruled out and Broadbent missed a

BELOW: The fans strike fear into Molineux hearts with a song!

sitter near the end so the score stayed 1-0. Forty-two thousand people were there to see Wolves tamed. The great Billy Wright admitted, 'Norris certainly had me worried,' and the press called the result the greatest giant-killing in the domestic game's history.

Cherries drew Spurs, second in the First Division, at home in round five. After Cox had seen Tottenham beat Sunderland 5-2 at White Hart Lane he was asked how his team would get on against such formidable opposition. He replied, 'I'm wondering who we'll be drawn against in the sixth round.' He was condemned for his 'stupid' prediction and even received a threatening letter signed by 20 Spurs supporters. There were forged tickets in circulation, hundreds were seized in a police raid in London, and the black market was thriving. There were just under 26,000 tickets available but many thousands more wanted in. An astonishing 19,500 turned up for a reserve game against Aldershot when tickets went on sale. Queues started building the night before. Spurs had Danny Blanchflower, Terry Medwin, Bobby Smith and Ted Ditchburn – but Cherries gave them a lesson. Ditchburn was particularly unsettled by Norris jumping up and down in front of him every time he went to kick the ball. The little inside-forward did the same at free-kicks and throw-ins. He was criticised for it but did nothing to contravene the rules

BELOW: Cup heroes, before the
Man Utd game: Godwin, Lyons,
Woollard, Clayton, Hughes,
Brown, Stiffle, Norris, Bedford,
Newsham, Cutler. United's team
was: Wood, Foulkes, Byrne,
Colman, Jones, McGuiness, Berry,
Whelan, Edwards, Viollet, Pegg

of the game. It was Norris, the 'nuisance', the 'secret weapon', who gave Cherries the lead on 13 minutes. Medwin equalised two minutes later. Then 10 minutes before the interval Newsham powered the home team back into the lead with a bullet header from Norris's cross. The crowd went berserk. One overexcited fan jumped on a linesman's foot, causing one of the sport's more unusual injury stoppages. A magnificent solo goal by Stiffle after 50 minutes gave the scoreline an almost unreal quality. Blanchflower did his best to rally Spurs, but it was too late.

Cherries had put out two of the top three teams in the country so there was an air of inevitability about the next round, with the First Division leaders and reigning champions Manchester United surely a little apprehensive about visiting Dean Court. United manager Matt Busby's right-hand man Jimmy 'Spud' Murphy watched Boscombe play a League match with Colchester. He said, 'That fitness they possess . . . phew!' The Bournemouth board decided to reward the supporters by pegging prices although the touts cashed in by selling 2s tickets for 35s. The directors, though, did have the good sense to launch their Million Penny Fund during the euphoric build-up to the game and the extra revenue helped pay for a gymnasium at the ground. The corporation at that time were spending £25,000 a year on promoting the town. They estimated the games against Wolves and Spurs had been worth £1m, and this when £1m was a lot of money. The Daily Echo said, 'Bournemouth by now has had as much publicity as Marilyn Monroe.' Although some things never change. The town certainly didn't have Monroe's young and vital image. The Echo said, 'Judging by the cartoons which have appeared in the national press recently, the typical Bournemouth resident is habitually immersed in rugs in a

ABOVE: Cartoon by Echo reader
Leslie Gold showing how to
counter Ollie Norris's tricks

ABOVE: Chairman Hayward with the legendary Matt Busby

LEFT: The players are mobbed following the United match

bathchair.' Even the (London) Times remarked that 'the retired colonels and ladies of Bournemouth must have been offered a new lease by Boscombe's achievements. This visual image of the residents of this town may have been true 30 years ago when H V Morton wrote of "the retired colonels with enlarged check-

RIGHT: Godwin and his defenders see off this United attack

LEFT: Stan Newsham scores with a header against. Tottenham – this superb image was captured by well-known photographer Harry Ashley long before auto-focus cameras became standard

coats and enlarged livers", but I doubt whether you could find enough retired colonels of the old tradition today to shake a stick at. A typical resident of 1957 is probably an estate agent or a motor car salesman.'

So the big day arrived, although not for the Bournemouth couple who postponed their wedding to be there to see the Busby Babes against Cox's Pippins. United were in with realistic hopes of a fantastic treble of League, FA Cup and European Cup. Tommy Taylor was ruled out through injury so mercurial teenager Duncan Edwards took his place up front. It would be a bit like replacing Alan Shearer with Ronaldo today. United goalkeeper Ray Wood played despite the pain of a boil in his left armpit. Record gate receipts, £3,370, from 28,799 spectators. Boscombe, wearing all-white (United were in blue), started nervously and Godwin's poor clearance presented an early chance to Edwards but the young superstar's shot cleared the bar. Norris collided with Mark Jones after 10 minutes. Ollie was hampered from then on by a leg injury but the United man was carried off, leaving the visitors down to 10 men for the rest of the first half. Brian Bedford, who would outwit defenders by dropping deep, hit the bar before finally bundling the ball into the net on 34 minutes, although it appeared that the ball had gone out of play from Stiffle's corner.

BELOW: Freddie Cox shows VIP guests around the new gymnasium

Jones came out for the second half but broke down again after just two minutes. Could Boscombe, with the extra man, hang on? Unfortunately not. The damage was done inside five minutes. Johnny Berry, at 29 the oldest of the Babes, equalised on the hour, with Cherries appealing for offside, and scored the winner from the penalty spot five minutes later after Dennis Viollet's snapshot hit Joe Brown and referee F B Coultas awarded a penalty. Brown came off and pointed to a mark on his shirt around a shoulder, claiming, 'That's where the ball hit me.' Skipper Hughes said, 'I thought it was harsh. Poor Joe couldn't get out of the way.' Echo reporter Alan Montgomery watched the newsreel film twice and claimed it was definitely not a penalty: 'In the film Brown is standing with his arms almost straight down to his sides. And he did not move those arms as the ball came whizzing towards him.' Montgomery, though, did not deny that United deserved to win. 'That lion-hearted player, by name Duncan Edwards, deserves a monument all to himself. His ceaseless energy in filling the gap left by the departure of Jones gave him the spirit of two men.' Of United, he wrote, 'Sheer soccer science, soccer perfection, their close passing in enemy territory spelt danger from the start.' Busby, in his book 'My Story', wrote: 'There were many great Cup occasions for United in 1956/7, yet I feel our finest hour was seen on the Dean Court ground at Bournemouth.' Less than a year on six of the United players that day – Edwards, Jones, Eddie Colman, Bill Whelan, Roger Byrne and David Pegg – were killed in an air crash at Munich. Thousands of Bournemouth supporters felt privileged to have seen them play.

A replay would have earned Boscombe £4,000 from a 60,000 crowd at Old Trafford. Instead they had to settle for the Giant-killer Cup, a new trophy inspired by their achievements and awarded by the Sunday Pictorial whose editor Colin Valdar wrote, 'We felt that the great pleasure and thrill given by Bournemouth to the whole nation should not go entirely unrewarded.'

ABOVE: The FA Cup that cheers ... Sheila Eaton remained a fan

ABOVE: Jo Brown conceded a controversial penalty against United

RIGHT: David Swindells with his
hit record, the Molineux Victory
Calypso, pictured in 1957

MEMORIES – Long-time supporter David Swindells was just 22 when
he recorded a musical tribute to the famous Cup run …

'I wrote the song on the back of an envelope on the train on the way
back from the Wolves game. It was called the Molineux Victory Calypso
and some friends and me went into a shop in Southbourne to record it.
My mates played accordion, bongos, maracas and guitar and I sang in
this awful pseudo West Indian accent. I thought I sounded like a stran-
gled cat, it was so embarrassing, but they played it at Dean Court and it
even went out on the BBC, radio and TV. It was just crazy for about
five weeks. It still makes me cringe, but, looking back, I suppose it was a
great deal of fun.'

41

Lighting Up Time

The fantastic FA Cup run of 1956/57 certainly distracted players and supporters alike from the League. Even so Cherries finished fifth, creating a new record for the most goals in a season (88 in the League, 16 in the Cup). Off the field a reconstituted Dean Court Supporters Club helped raise enough funds to wipe out a £10,000 overdraft within a year. The supporters also chipped in with money for new terracing at the Brighton Beach End. Freddie Cox was very hot property and was strongly linked with Orient and Burnley. At a dinner given in the club's honour by the Bournemouth Hotel and Boarding-House Association, the BHBA's J H Petterson called Cox, 'this new and most important import to the town . . . that atom bomb, that example of nuclear energy.' But it was to be very much a case of 'after the Lord Mayor's show' for Cherries whose recent achievements had been marked with another dinner, a full-blown civic affair, at the Pavilion theatre.

ABOVE: Arriving at Bradford in 1960, suitably attired for unfamiliar harsh northern climes

Maybe it was the rich food at all these slap-up dinners. Maybe it was complacency, but 1957/58 was a let-down.

Ever since their formation Boscombe had never had to venture further north than Mansfield, apart from in the FA Cup. That was about to change. The Football League, after four years of dithering, decided at their annual meeting in summer 1957 on the first major change for 36 years. The geographical divide was to be scrapped in favour of the formation of a new fourth division the following season. Clubs finishing in the top half of their section would be in Division Three, those in the bottom half in Four. So season 1957/58 was a cut-throat slog with clubs battling it out to finish 'above the line', ie in the top 12. Adventurous Boscombe struggled to adapt to safety-first football. In November a flu bug left Bournemouth with just seven fit players from a squad of 26 and three games had to be called off. The following month they crashed out of the Cup at Northampton and Cox had a fall-out with the media, taking the Echo's Alan Montgomery to task over his report on that game. The manager said, 'I expect criticism at all times but I think I am entitled to fair and constructive criticism.' Oh dear. There would be a similar bust-up some years later.

Southampton, with a young Terry Paine in their ranks, tonked seven without reply at The Dell to inflict Bournemouth's worst League defeat to that point. It also sent them into the dreaded bottom half. Newsham, leading scorer for the past three seasons, had gone to Notts County for £10,000, and was replaced by Dickie Dowsett, from Southampton. More money from the supporters club was spent on new players and the season ended with the club in ninth position, comfortably in the top half and assured of a Division Three place. Parkstone-born Jimmy White made his debut at centre-forward in the final game of the season, at home to Port Vale, at the age of 15 years 10 months and 17 days, the

ABOVE: Dickie Dowsett ... joined from Southampton to replace Stan Newsham in attack

youngest ever. Cox was keen on youth development. He released Stiffle, 30, in the close season and brought in a 22-year-old from Ringwood Town, Ray Bumstead, who would go on to make 412 League appearances over the next 11 years. With Ronnie Bolton also arriving as part of the latest rebuilding exercise there was surprise over the timing more than anything when Cox finally gave in to the temptation to try his hand at a higher level and left to run First Division Portsmouth. Don Welsh, an ex-Charlton and England player with managerial experience at Brighton and Liverpool, took over. Dean Court fans had their first chance to see northern clubs like Bury, Stockport, Hull, Rochdale, Doncaster and Chesterfield – and the home record was excellent with nine wins, two draws and two defeats. But it was a different story away, with Cherries losing 11 of their 13 games and picking up just three points on their travels. The northern air obviously didn't suit them. No such excuse in the FA Cup, though, where Bournemouth were sent packing by Isthmian League amateurs Tooting and Mitcham.

The 60th anniversary season, 1959/60, was another average campaign. Cherries scored 72 times, but conceded 72 as well. They were mid-table all the way. Their away form was again poor. What made it worse for Bournemouth supporters was the fact that Southampton won the Third Division title. In 14 meet-

ABOVE: Ray Bumstead, rode in to town from Ringwood

BELOW LEFT: Another local boy, Jimmy White from Parkstone, with his dad (right) and manager Freddie Cox

BELOW: Let there be light . . . work begins on erecting floodlights at the South End

ings up to that time between the two clubs Saints had won seven to Cherries' four with three drawn. The 1950s ended with the club talking about erecting floodlights and mulling over the expense – £2,000 to lay a cable from Holdenhurst Road, between £8,000 and £10,000 for the lights themselves. The lights did go up but the 60s didn't start too brightly. The introduction of the League Cup was certainly no big deal for Bournemouth, a bye in the first round followed by a replay defeat at Crewe. Crowds were down, the team were battling relegation and Welsh was under fire from the fans. He hit back with a verbal attack on spectators who shouted 'Get rid of it' or 'Get into him'. He said, 'Spectators, I feel, spoil and mar more players than they make and they do it by shouting the wrong advice at the wrong time.' He also felt ball-players were being driven out by the increased speed at which football was being

TOP LEFT: Fifty years' service, man and boy ... Reg Hayward

TOP RIGHT: Bill McGarry signs in

ABOVE: Don Welsh

RIGHT: Photocall, 1963-64

45

played. Welsh also had to contend with the threat of a players' strike over contracts and the maximum wage in November 1960. The Boscombe players' delegate was Bryn Jones, brother of Spurs' better-known Cliff. Welsh said he would use amateurs if necessary. This same month marked the death of Reg Hayward, who had been chairman since 1947, a director since 1942. He started working at the club before the First World War, making deliveries on his bike, and served the Cherries for 50 of his 63 years. Results failed to improve and Welsh was sacked a year later. His replacement was Bill McGarry, the club's first player-manager.

ABOVE: High-profile supporter Ken Baily lived in Boscombe and was also England's unofficial cheerleader

ABOVE: Joe Brown pictured at
Old Trafford in the 1970s

MEMORIES – Joe Brown went on to manage Burnley and was chief
scout and youth coach and development officer at Manchester United
where he worked with young players like Norman Whiteside, Mark
Hughes, the Neville brothers and David Beckham before they became
famous . . .

'The six years I spent at Bournemouth were the happiest of my career.
We had a good time under Jack Bruton and it was even more exciting
with Freddie Cox. Unfortunately, it wasn't quite as exciting with Don
Welsh! Before moving south I was at Middlesbrough with Ollie Norris
and Mr Bruton asked me about him before signing him. Aah . . . the Cup
run. Wolves, when Reg Cutler ended up in the net and pulled the goal-
post down. We scored and somehow held on. The best match was
Tottenham. They thought we would be easy meat, but they were wrong.
As for United, we competed well against them. I remember their winner very well. Johnny Berry had a shot and Tommy Godwin charged it
down with his knees. I ran back to the goal line and when the ball came
back in I chested it down. It hit me just above my heart. But the ref gave
a penalty and that was it. Still, we had a good run. The town was in a
state of excitement for about two months. The place was alive,
bubbling, it was like a constant carnival.'

CHAPTER 7

Mac to Mac

Bill McGarry had captained Huddersfield for eight years and won four England caps. He played right-half and inspired a recovery to 40 points and 19th place, just enough to stay up. His first full season in charge opened with an unbeaten run of 14 games including the first visit to Fratton Park since 1923/24, Dickie Dowsett scoring in a 1-1 draw. In the first week of October, in a game which started 50 minutes late because the new floodlights failed (this was well before scandals involving Far Eastern betting syndicates) Cherries beat Notts County 5-1 to go top of the table. A month later, also at Dean Court, non-league Margate won with embarrassing ease in the FA Cup. It would be almost 10 years before Cherries exacted emphatic revenge for that 3-0 defeat. But McGarry's men pushed all the way in the League, even beating eventual champions Portsmouth before 22,940 fans at home, before eventually miss-

LEFT: Bill McGarry heads clear

RIGHT: Simply the Best ... Dave clutches number one slot

ing out to Grimsby, who did the double over them. The manager was linked with Derby but stayed to mount another promotion push in 1962/63. Cherries drew too many games, especially at home, and the big freeze saw the club go nine weeks without a game.

The season didn't finish until the end of May, with Boscombe in fifth. Godwin went to Dorchester in the close season with brilliant young goalkeeper Dave Best, just 16, moving in from Wareham Rangers. McGarry, one of the game's most coveted young managers, went to Watford. Reg Flewin arrived as manager from Stockport and got away to a flying start with his team dropping just one point in their first seven League games and soaring to the top of the table. Then they won just one of their next seven. Flewin wheeled and dealed but once again Cherries just missed out on promotion, finishing in fourth spot. The following season, 1964/65, was disappointing. Ronnie Bolton's dismissal against Northampton in the League Cup provoked a torrent of cushions from the Main Stand, a police escort for the referee and a rebuke from the Football League, followed by meek surrender to Bristol City at home in the FA Cup. Attendances plummeted and once again there was talk of financial problems. Season 1965/66, which saw the introduction of substitutes, started with Flewin in a London hospital and Cherries going down 1-0 at home to Walsall. They failed to

score in 21 of their League games and only once managed to score more than two. Burnley pulverised Bournemouth 7-0 in the FA Cup third round replay, Andy Lochead scoring five. Maybe the players missed the rousing influence of Field-Marshal Bernard Montgomery, who had visited them in the dressing-room before the home game which ended 1-1.

Ill-health forced Flewin to resign and Cox returned for a second spell in charge late in 1965. Long-serving Dai Woodward ended his association as player and trainer dating back to just after the Second World War. His replacement was another stalwart, John Kirk. Cox reshuffled the squad, bringing back with him from Gillingham an older Jimmy White (although still only 24), David Stocks and Rodney Taylor. A good start to the campaign failed to attract crowds above 7,000. The turning point came in October when Cherries, the leaders, met second-placed QPR at Dean Court. Rangers won 3-1 (and also went on to take the title as well as appearing in the League Cup final at Wembley, the first Division Three side to do so). It was downhill from there for Boscombe. By Christmas gates had dipped below 4,000 and they won just two out of their next 23 games to finish the season precariously close to the relegation zone. From 11th in 1964/65 to 18th in 1965/66 to 20th in 1966/67, with just 77 goals in the past two seasons, the Sixties were far from swinging at Dean Court. England had won the World Cup but the feelgood factor failed to filter down to Bournemouth. Another largely depressing season was memo-

TOP LEFT: Field Marshal Bernard Montgomery meets Doug Hayward (centre) and Roy Gater (right)

TOP: Freddie Cox returns to Dean Court and considers tactics

ABOVE: Ronnie Bolton came out worse in collision with Ron Yeats

ABOVE: 1966 and all that . . . England's World Cup win couldn't inspire this Cherries team

BELOW: The new floodlights offer an unusual vantage point

rable for one game, at home to Liverpool in the FA Cup third round. There were more than 24,000 inside the ground to see Bill Shankly's men put under the cosh for pretty much the entire 90 minutes. Keith East had what seemed to be a good goal disallowed and Liverpool, including Tommy Smith, Emlyn Hughes, Ian Callaghan, Ian St John and World Cup winner Roger Hunt, hung on for a no-score draw. Ronnie Bolton suffered a terrible head injury in a collision with Ron Yeats – he asked trainer Kirk to stick a plaster on it so he could go back out, but instead he was hospitalised. 'Shanks' joked that his men had given the hard-up Third Division side the chance of a money-spinning replay. Bournemouth started brightly in the game at Anfield but Tony Hateley headed Liverpool in front and further goals followed from Thompson, Hunt and Lawler.

Cherries finished in mid-table and former striker Dickie Dowsett returned to run the Cherry Bees fund-raising scheme which aimed to generate £30,000 a year, while the new £16,000 supporters club opened in time for the new season. Saturday home games in September kicked off at 7.30pm so that holiday-makers as well as parks footballers could attend. Cox was still keen on youth development and Boscombe's youngsters returned from a 10-team tournament in Rotterdam as runners-up. The manager was given a five-year contract and the senior players offered improved terms.

A settled team and good home form kept Cherries firmly in the promotion frame. But defender Roy Gater's move to Crewe in the New Year seemed to upset the team's shape, the away form was not good enough and just four wins in the last 16 games meant Bournemouth had to settle for fourth place, which sounds respectable, but they were 10 points behind third-placed Luton. In the summer of 1969 Cox signed three strikers. He faced stiff competition to get Trevor Hartley, already a fully-qualified coach at just 22, from West Ham for £5,000 and swapped Ken Pound for the experienced John Meredith from Gillingham. The other forward arrived from York City for a bargain £10,000. Ted MacDougall, 22, a former newspaper print worker from Inverness, had started out at Liverpool but was unable to dislodge stars like Hunt and St John from the first team. Cox said, 'Ted can finish moves off and players like that are rare. If we had possessed someone in the forward line who could take advantage of the chances created we would have gone up last season. He is a constructive player and particularly strong in the air.' The supporters would soon find out just how strong.

ABOVE: Supermac arrives on the scene . . . Ted MacDougall

ABOVE: David Stocks lets fly in
his 1960s heyday at Dean Court

MEMORIES – Former Cherries defender David Stocks, who returned
to Bournemouth after retiring from the game to work as a financial
adviser. . .

'Freddie Cox signed me from Gillingham. Myself, Roy Gater and goalkeeper Roger Jones were always the first three names on the
teamsheet. The other players used to call us Freeman, Hardy and
Willis, after the shoe shop. Ted MacDougall was a selfish sort of player, even in training he would try to smash the ball into the net rather
than pass. Phil Boyer was a great footballer, very under-rated. Bondy
got him and Ted to switch and draw defenders out of position. It was
simple but very effective. Tony Scott was a brilliant crosser of a ball,
he'd curve it with the outside of his foot, even from corner kicks.
When I got injured Bondy brought in Mel Machin, he could do magical
things with a football, and I left to captain Torquay.'

CHAPTER 8

My Name's Bond, John Bond

The new forwards, MacDougall included, initially failed to add much in the way of fire power. Cherries won just two of their opening 17 League games although they did well in the League Cup, beating Bristol Rovers and First Division Sheffield Wednesday before going out to Leicester in round three. Cox slipped up with the sale of England Under 23 goalkeeper Roger Jones, for a paltry £30,000 to Blackburn, when he didn't have adequate cover. Cherries plunged into the relegation zone but thought they had done enough to secure safety when they returned from rivals Gillingham with a point. The Gills, however, won their final game at champions Orient – and consigned Bournemouth to relegation for the first time, on goal average.

The new chairman Harold Walker, a lifelong fan and a director for three years, was bitterly disappointed. When he took over his aim was to make Boscombe 'the Newcastle of the South' and they were heading in the wrong direction. Cox was fired and the job was offered to Cyril Lea, but the Ipswich man took too long to make up his mind so Walker turned to the flam-

FAR LEFT: Ambitious ... new chairman Harold Walker

LEFT: John Bond welcomes Keith Miller (left) to Dean Court

TOP: Celebrating promotion from Division Four at the end of the 1970/71 season

ABOVE: Classy young defender Mel Machin strides into action

boyant E-type Jag-driving cigar-chomping John Bond, formerly coach at Gillingham. Bondy didn't rate MacDougall at first, but, along with coach Ken Brown and assistant manager Reg Tyrell, introduced new-style training techniques which allowed the players to express themselves on and off the field, helping to bring the best out of Supermac and the rest of the squad. Bond and Walker wanted to give the club a more Continental feel so changed the name to AFC Bournemouth and introduced red and black striped shirts in honour of AC Milan. A distinctive new badge, still used today, became known as 'Dickie Dowsett's head'. Goalkeeper Fred Davies, from Cardiff, and Keith Miller, for a bargain £10,000 from West Ham, gave the side a solid spine. Miller, a former teammate of Bond's, made just one full appearance for the Hammers, against Leeds, and it was his hard but perfectly fair tackle that led to Paul Reaney breaking a leg, ruling the full-back out of the 1970 World Cup. Winger Tony Scott added flair and provided the ammunition for MacDougall to blow away practically every defence placed in his unerring sights. Seven successive wins took Bournemouth to the top of the table, MacDougall had scored 16 times by the end of October then smashed six past Oxford City in the FA Cup to set a new club record. A classy young full-back called Mel Machin joined from Gillingham for £9,000, and Phil Boyer, who proved to be the perfect foil for Supermac, signed for £20,000 following drawn-out negotiations with York. It didn't take Boyer long to decide to join, however. He walked from Bournemouth train station to Dean Court through pouring rain and signed on the dotted line within 15 minutes of his arrival, still drenched. Bond said, 'I had to sign him because Ted was constantly telling me what a good player he was and how they had worked together at York. Phil, basically, is a manager's dream.' Boyer described his understanding with MacDougall as 'a kind of telepathy', while Chelsea star Peter Osgood, writing in a national newspaper, said, 'Ted has lived like a lord off Phil's service. Ted would only be 70 per cent as good without him.' Bournemouth bounced back up at the first attempt, finishing third, with MacDougall hitting 49 goals, more than anyone else in the League and easily breaking Ronnie Eyre's 40-year-old record.

ABOVE: The scoreboard says it all

Bond's dream machine rolled on the following season, 1971/72, scorching to the top of the Third Division, with MacDougall putting the town on the map with a staggering nine goals (including four headers and a penalty) in the 11-0 FA Cup annihilation of Margate. The visitors' manager jokingly pleaded with Bond to take Supermac off at half-time, The Sunday People re-named him MacDougoal and the Observer described him as, 'The most highly-rated piece of property in Bournemouth's rich acres,' adding, in a reference to an Everton legend, 'real Dixie stuff.' Bond estimated that one game put £50,000 on his value and MacDougall was selected to appear alongside Eusebio, Jimmy Johnstone and Uwe Seeler for a European XI in Geoff Hurst's testimonial. Walker's high ambition seemed within reach, with crowds of up to 22,000 cramming into Dean Court to watch exciting, attacking football. Bond splashed out £200,000 in his first 18 months in charge. He usually bought players he knew well from his former clubs, especially Torquay, whose decimated squad were relegated to Division Four in 1972. One group of Torquay fans even followed their favourite players to Dean Court! Bond's poaching

BELOW: Perfect foil . . . Phil Boyer

ABOVE: Supermac's famous diving
header at Villa Park

habit didn't unduly bother Cherries supporters at the time, but would do later. The team looked poised for a second successive promotion, but were let down by a late sequence of six games without a win, including a highly-charged 1-1 home draw with Brighton, who nipped in to clinch second place. Once again MacDougall was the League's highest scorer, with 35. Big clubs, including Wolves, West Ham and Coventry, were sniffing around, and Scotland manager Tommy Docherty had the striker closely scrutinised. But Supermac – very much in the national spotlight following his superb diving header against Aston Villa in front of the Match of the Day cameras and 48,000 spectators (a Third Division crowd record which stood until Sheffield Wednesday broke it in 1980) – claimed he was happy to honour his contract, especially as he had business interests in the area with sports shops in Bournemouth and Poole. Bond, too, rejected an offer from Coventry to become their manager, and swooped during the close-season to sign two more players who would go on, like Machin, to become hugely influential in the club's future. Ex-Scottish international Jimmy Gabriel moved 30 miles down the road from Southampton, while winger Harry Redknapp travelled the well-worn path from West Ham for a then club record £31,000.

This was a Himalayan high point in the club's history. Bournemouth were installed as pre-season promotion favourites for 1972/73 and the chairman unveiled plans for what would become known as the Walker Stand, a £1 million redevelopment of the Brighton Beach End with a multi-sports complex beneath. Everything looked fine on paper – but football has always been

ABOVE: Boyer on target again

played on grass (or, for a brief, unlamented period, Astroturf). Cherries took just one point from their first three games. Despite an 11-game unbeaten run which lifted them to second place by mid-October, more cynical supporters felt the bubble may be about to burst. It didn't happen that quickly, but it did deflate, gradually, inexorably. MacDougall, earning £150 a week and perhaps unsettled by months of speculation, was linked with Crystal Palace, Terry Venables' so-called 'Team of the Seventies', then signed for Manchester United for £200,000, a record for a Third Division player. He had netted a phenomenal 126 goals in 165 appearances during his three years at the club. Bond, whose first impressions of MacDougall couldn't have been more wrong, pleaded with him to stay, saying, 'I'm happy for Ted, heartbroken for the club and disappointed for myself.' As it turned out, the move to Old Trafford was a disaster for everyone concerned. United were struggling to adjust to life after the near-holy trinity of Best, Law and Charlton; Mac wasn't so super after all at such a rarefied level (he lasted just 150 days with United); and Bournemouth simply couldn't replace him. Bond used half the money to sign two strikers, Brian Clark (valued at a record £70,000) and Ian Gibson, from Cardiff, then became embroiled in a row with Notts County over midfield star Don Masson, which ended with County unsuccessfully issuing a writ over Bournemouth's conduct in the deal. Clark got off to a flying start, scoring four

BELOW: Tony Scott, a regular supplier of quality crosses

ABOVE: Supermac reigned
supreme in the air

BELOW: Best of pals, Ted
MacDougall and Phil Boyer

times in the 7-2 win at Rotherham, a record away win which
still stands. Another new signing, winger Alan Groves, scored
twice. In November Bond signed a 10-year contract reputed-
ly worth £100,000, making him one of the highest-paid managers outside the First Division, and described his relationship
with the chairman as the best in the League.

MEMORIES – Ted MacDougall, voted all-time best player ...
'I don't think Freddie Cox had seen me play before he signed me from
York. I drove down with my wife and our pet dog and we couldn't
afford a hotel so we slept in the car. We were relegated in my first season, even though I got 25 goals. Then Bondy arrived and we had a big
row because he wanted me to play on the right wing. I knew what my
strength was, and that was scoring goals, so he worked with me on
near-post runs and stuff like that, things that no one else had done
before, and I ended up with 49 goals and the side went straight back up.
I wasn't that tall but I used to hang in the air. And I was quite brave.
Also, when the ball was in the air I couldn't miscontrol it! The game I
remember is the one at Aston Villa, in front of 48,000 people. My goal
was shown over and over again on TV and it ended up goal of the season. We finished third that year and just missed out and the team started to break up. They all played in the First Division (now the
Premiership) which shows just how strong we were and what we could
have achieved if we had stayed together. But the momentum was gone
and I felt it was time to move on. I certainly didn't do it for the money, I
was well paid at Bournemouth and only got another tenner a week at
Old Trafford. I have very fond memories of my time at Bournemouth,
it's where I made my name. I was very single-minded, selfish if you like,
on the pitch and on the training ground. I loved playing with guys like
Tony Scott and Phil Boyer, we complemented each other perfectly. And
Bondy was the best coach I ever worked with, we had a sort of father-
son love-hate relationship. I still love Bournemouth to bits and I really
hope they do well. I think they would do better at a higher level
because they like to play football.'

CHAPTER 9

Mass Exodus

Cherries were top in January 1973, but their habit of slipping up against less-fancied teams saw them narrowly miss out on promotion for a second successive season. Former manager Freddie Cox died aged 52 following a heart attack in the summer. Progress was slow on the Walker Stand, or, to give it its proper name, the Sports Centre Stand. But Bournemouth, as expected, were very much in the running for promotion as Christmas loomed. John Bond, however, frustrated at having just missed out twice on promotion to Division Two and sorely tempted to try his hand at a higher level, was aware that First Division Norwich City, who were prepared to pay £10,000 compensation, wanted him to take over at Carrow Road. One of Bond's final flourishes had been to send the players out for their FA Cup third round tie at Newcastle in March carrying placards saying 'Our aim – to entertain.' Cherries lost 2-0, but lived up to their pre-match promise. The close-season tour to Iran, New Caledonia, Australia, New Zealand and Tahiti very nearly ended in tragedy, as Jimmy Gabriel explained: 'It was very, very hot in New Caledonia (a Pacific island off the east coast of Australia) so obviously the lads went down to the beach a few times to cool off. There was all the usual horseplay and mucking about. It seemed so natural. But we noticed while we were there that each day a couple of ladies came down with their kids, and while the youngsters were allowed to play on the sand, none of them ever set foot in the water. The ladies kept themselves to themselves, and so did we, but on the last day we started talking to them. We asked one woman why they never went for a swim, even though it was so hot. The answer took

BELOW: Popular winger Alan Groves died young

ABOVE: Trevor Hartley ...
youngest boss in the League

BELOW: John Benson (centre,
front) and Fred Davies (right, back
row) took over managerial duties

our breath away. She said, "We don't swim because there are little fish in this bay with spines. If you step on them you will be dead in three seconds." We just stood there with our mouths open. The whole team could have been wiped out.' No such hazards awaited Bond in Norfolk. Walker wanted him to stay (although he wasn't prepared to increase his wages) and so did the fans. But Norwich were determined. Bond's departure was to rip the heart out of Cherries. Walker said he was 'sick and flabbergasted' and felt as if he'd been kicked in the stomach. Bond took coach Ken Brown with him, closely followed by Machin, Davies and John Benson. That was just the start. Bournemouth dropped out of the promotion picture, and the growing tide of anti-Bond feeling among the supporters was fuelled by the sale of Boyer, for £150,000, to Norwich of course, where he linked up again with MacDougall. (The Canaries were later fined £1,000 for making an illegal approach.) Trevor Hartley, promoted from reserve team duties to first team coach, at 27 the youngest in the League, upset supporters by offloading the popular Alan Groves to Oldham, where he sadly suffered a

fatal heart attack, aged just 30. (By a tragic coincidence, Groves' best pal at Dean Court, Mickey Cave, was later to die young and tragically in America.) Hartley was also criticised for making his brother-in-law Bobby Howe his assistant. Just one win in their last 16 games sent Cherries sliding down the table. Tony Powell became the sixth player to follow Bond to Carrow Road, closely followed by the former manager's son, Kevin. Poor results at the start of the following season, culminating in an embarrassing FA Cup defeat by non-league Wycombe, spelt the end for Hartley. Benson returned as player-manager following Tony Nelson's brief spell as caretaker boss. He couldn't save the club from relegation. Construction work on the Walker Stand was halted. The steel girder skeleton was left to rust and eventually pulled down. Back in the Fourth Division, Bournemouth boasted a promising strike pair, Burley-born Kevin Reeves and Howard Goddard, who struck 27 goals between them. But just three wins in the 14-game run-in wiped out any thoughts of bouncing back at the first attempt, and the razzle-dazzle days of the Bond era seemed an eternity away. Crowds were down and money was tight. Goddard was released to raise much-needed cash, and the reserve team was scrapped. England youth international Mark Nightingale moved to Crystal Palace while a youngster called Graham Roberts was also released. Within five years Roberts was a regular for Spurs and England and youth team boss Harry Redknapp later described the decision to release him as 'the stupidest for many years.'

Benson hauled himself off the bench the following season to forge a reliable central defensive partnership with John Impey, but erratic performances and poor crowds meant that another gem had to be sold to help balance the books, with Reeves heading to Norwich (where else?) for £50,000. Within three years he would play for England and move to Manchester City for £1 million. Cherries went six games unbeaten at the end of the season but could only finish mid-table. Another local prospect, Steve Gritt, went to Charlton on the cheap. The free-spending days were long gone. Benson tried to strengthen his squad with free transfer and loan signings for the 1977/78 season but Bournemouth spent most of the campaign struggling to stay out of the re-election dogfight and somehow hauled

BELOW: Alec Stock brought pride and dignity to the club

BOTTOM: Goalkeeper Ian Leigh

themselves up to 17th in the final countdown. The following season offered the prospect of a rare local derby, with Portsmouth, fallen on even harder times and forced to slum it in the Fourth Division for the first time in their illustrious history. Over 10,000 fans turned up at Dean Court to see the home team overturn the promotion favourites 3-1, a result which lifted them into the top six. But normal service was resumed with defeat against Aldershot, triggering another slide down the table.

Supermac returned on a free transfer from Southampton, ironically on the same day that the club received an additional £22,500 after a High Court ruling against Manchester United over the striker's initial move. MacDougall failed to score on his homecoming against Hartlepool. Instead it was Mick Butler who got both goals in a 2-2 draw. A terrible sequence of results finally persuaded Benson to quit early in the New Year. He cited the mounting pressure on his family. Bobby Moore and Rodney Marsh, both looking to break into management, were touted as successors, but the job went to the highly-respected Alec Stock. He vowed to bring back 'pride and dignity' and began with a bang, a 7-1 league win over Doncaster, the club's best for 22 years.

MacDougall scored twice against Rovers, but never really looked like hitting the hot streak that had lit up the town a few years before. The fans thought the glory days may be about to return but were disappointed once again as Bournemouth finished 18th. Stock rang the changes the following season. Even Supermac was

BELOW: Under attack . . . Kenny Allen in big win at Tranmere

ABOVE: Little terror . . . Tony Funnell joined from Brentford

RIGHT: Dave Webb takes charge

dropped for a short spell, while Keith Miller, virtually ever-present for nine seasons, made way for the promising young Phil Ferns. A Friday night game at Tranmere in late September was memorable for two reasons – Cherries won 5-0, their first victory in six games, and goalkeeper Kenny Allen was attacked by an elderly Tranmere fan wielding a walking-stick. MacDougall, with, by his standards, a paltry 16-goal return from over 50 games in his second spell at Dean Court, moved to Blackpool as Alan Ball's assistant. England cricket legend Ian Botham, who was not quite in the same class as a footballer, made his league debut as a sub for Scunthorpe in the 3-3 draw at Dean Court. Another season over, another mid-table finish. Former Chelsea star Dave Webb was brought in as coach and soon promoted to manager as Stock moved on to the board and AFC Bournemouth eased into the 1980s without anyone outside the town taking too much notice. The 1981/82 season kicked off with three points for a win and Cherries won six of their first nine games. Former Arsenal star Eddie Kelly was brought in to strengthen midfield and striker Tony Funnell arrived for £5,000, although Webb apparently offered the Brentford chairman a nice little motor instead. Ian Leigh, replacing injured giant Kenny Allen in goal, and Milton Graham made a big impact as the side strung together a few wins to finally mount a sustained promotion challenge. Ex-Arsenal icon Charlie George flitted in and out, playing just two games before he returned to Derby. Another high-profile figure, comedian Jim Davidson, a friend of Webb's, joined the board for a while and would fly in for games by helicopter. With Funnell and Trevor Morgan doing well up front, tenacious full-back Tommy Heffernan inspiring the defence and Nigel Spackman belying his tender years to help link it all together, the town at last had a team to be proud of again.

Fourth place and promotion was clinched with a draw at Bradford City, who also went up. Both sets of fans joined together in celebration. Webb, who had briefly but sensationally quit the club in February, only to be talked into returning a week later, was immediately linked with bigger teams. They don't come much bigger than Manchester United, although at that time the Reds were going through a pretty barren patch.

TOP: Milton Graham scored some important goals for Cherries

ABOVE: Tough-tackling Tommy Heffernan starred in defence

TOP: George Best and Brian Tiler compare beards

ABOVE: George Best runs out for his debut against Newport

ABOVE RIGHT: Trevor Morgan celebrates another goal

The two sides met in the Milk (formerly League) Cup – United won 2-0 at Old Trafford and drew the second-leg 2-2 at Dean Court where Ray Wilkins was stretchered off with a shattered cheekbone. But the United games were little more than a money-spinning sideshow as disappointing League results belied early-season optimism. It still came as a shock when Webb was sacked and coach Harry Redknapp became caretaker boss. The players were demoralised and slumped to a record 9-0 defeat at Lincoln, closely followed by a 5-0 thumping at Orient. It wasn't an auspicious start for Redknapp, a naturally chirpy, confident character in the Webb mould. 'I thought about jacking it in after the game at Lincoln,' said Redknapp. 'The pitch was frozen solid and our players didn't have the right studs. Two of them fell over just running out of the tunnel and I knew straight away it wasn't going to be our day.' Cherries went two months

without a win before beating Brentford 4-3 on New Year's Day 1983, with Funnell recalled to lead the attack against his former club. Pressure was mounting on chairman Walker, who sold his majority shareholding to Guernsey-based Wigbourne Holdings to wipe out the club's £500,000 debt. Adminstration and financial affairs were put in the control of former Aston Villa player Brian Tiler, described as a consultant, and ex-Sheffield Wednesday defender Don Megson took over as manager with Redknapp reverting to coaching duties. It soon emerged that entrepeneur Anton Johnson – described in the press as a millionaire, the King of Clubs, the Mr Fix-It of Football – was behind the takeover and the deal had been hush-hush to hide his involvement from the League. He had already been involved in similar deals at Rotherham and Southend in contravention of the ruling body's regulations. Not for the first time, and certainly not the last, events off the pitch overshadowed those on it. The takeover controversy dragged on for nearly a year with Johnson offering to sell the club back to Walker, before local builder Rodney Barton brought ownership back to the town in January 1984. Before that happened, though, one of arch-publicist Johnson's masterstrokes had been persuading George Best, one of the greatest footballers of all time, to turn out for Bournemouth. The faded genius made his debut, overweight, unfit, his once-handsome face half-hidden by a heavy beard, in

ABOVE: Now it's Don Megson in charge (centre, middle row) with coach Harry Redknapp sitting on his left side

front of twice-the-average crowd. There were glimpses of the old magic but Best couldn't stave off defeat against Newport. Predictably, he failed to turn up for the next two games although he did play four more times before being released at the end of the season, when Cherries ended their first campaign back in the Third Division in 14th place.

Once again cash flow problems forced a summer clear-out sale, with Spackman, an effective rather than eye-catching midfielder who had failed to capture the fans' imagination, and Heffernan leaving for a meagre combined total of just £55,000. Tiler defended the deals as fans protested, and a little-known striker called Ian Thompson joined for just £16,000 from Salisbury City. The 1983/84 season started badly and Megson oiled the wheels of the managerial merry-go-round by resigning. Redknapp, after much deliberation, took over. Better times were just around the corner.

BELOW: Keith Miller in action

MEMORIES – Keith Miller played 428 games, scoring 19 goals, for Cherries in 10 seasons, including four when he was ever-present. Still living in the Bournemouth area, he is sales manager for a magazine … 'I cost £10,000 from West Ham when I joined in 1970, so that works out at £1,000 a season. I averaged over 40 games a season, so I reckon they got their money's worth out of me. John Benson said the older I got the better I became and when Alec Stock was manager he brought me back into the side to give it more bite. I maybe didn't have the skill of some of the other players but I made up for it in commitment. I wore every shirt apart from the goalkeeper's, but I only had one game at number nine – scoring goals wasn't my strong point! It was a great honour to captain the side to promotion for the first time in our history during my first season. The following season, 1971/72, was heart-breaking. We finished third behind Villa and Brighton and everyone said we were the best Bournemouth team up to that point. The Villa game where Ted scored the diving header was memorable, so was Margate, even though it was too one-sided to be a good game. But one I wish I could forget was at Northampton in 1976. We were 6-0 down at half-time. At least they didn't score any more!'

Champions!

Harry Redknapp, whose first brief taste of management a year before had been a distinctly underwhelming experience, remained under pressure in the League despite bringing defender and crowd favourite Roger Brown back from Fulham for £40,000 for a second spell. But there was welcome relief in the FA Cup. Walsall were beaten 4-0 in the first round,

BELOW: Paul Morrell skips over a tackle by Aston Villa's David Platt

ABOVE: Ian Thompson wheels away in delight after scoring against Manchester United

BELOW: Defender Roger Brown returned to Bournemouth for a successful second spell

before a goalless draw at Windsor and Eton. Then came a massive incentive – Cherries would play Manchester United at home if they could beat the non-league side in the replay. Mission duly accomplished, albeit in a dour 2-0 sort of way, almost 15,000 supporters packed into Dean Court for the glamorous third round tie. United were managed by Ron Atkinson and boasted a host of internationals including Ray Wilkins, Bryan Robson, Frank Stapleton, Norman Whiteside and Arnold Muhren. Cherries, on the other hand, were without captain John Beck because of flu while stand-in skipper Brown was returning after a four-match absence. Brown, Phil Brignull and Chris Sulley were outstanding at the back. Ian Leigh made a brilliant save from Arthur Graham and three minutes later, on the hour, another, less well-known Graham, Milton, capitalised on Gary Bailey's mistake to put the home team ahead. Thompson pounced on a mistake by Robson to score a superb second just two minutes later – and United were out. Atkinson kept his expensive flops in the dressing-room for almost an hour after the game and called them 'a disgrace.' He could have been more gracious towards Bournemouth who once again put the town on the map. Another colourful manager, Malcolm Allison, lay in wait in the fourth round. This time there was to be no fairytale as his Second Division Middlesbrough won 2-0 at Ayresome Park.

Back in the League Bournemouth were struggling. Redknapp brought in Fulham's Eire international Sean O'Driscoll, initially on loan, and veteran striker Billy Rafferty arrived from Portsmouth to replace Bristol City-bound Trevor Morgan. Rafferty made an immediate impression, scoring twice on his debut to set up a 3-0 win over Walsall, a game which was to prove the turning point as his new club climbed to safety. O'Driscoll would go on to make a more significant contribution in the long-term, setting the club record for most appearances and eventually graduating to first team coach. Cherries finished 17th in the League but this was the season when they finally won some more silverware. A new competition for clubs in the lower two divisions, the Associate Members Cup, was divided into the old geographical sections for the first few rounds – Bournemouth beat Aldershot,

Wrexham, Bristol Rovers and Millwall to clinch a place in the final against northern section winners Hull City. The game was played at Hull's Boothferry Park and the Tigers started as favourites but it was Roger Brown who lifted the trophy following a fine 2-1 victory with goals by Poole-born Paul Morrell and Milton Graham. (The competition would later be known by several different names, according to whoever was sponsoring it, and all subsequent finals were played at Wembley. Bournemouth's big day out at the national stadium was still to come.)

Former Cherries striker Mickey Cave was found dead from carbon monoxide poisoning at his home in Pennsylvania. He was 35. Cave had two spells with Bournemouth before leaving to join the Seattle Sounders in America where he linked up with former colleagues Redknapp, Gabriel, Howe and Steve Buttle. His name lives on in the supporters' Player of the Year Trophy sponsored by the Echo. A slow start to the 1984/85 season was followed by a run of nine wins in 11 games which lifted Cherries to the fringe of the promotion places by December. A barren Christmas and a dismal February eventually consigned them to mid-table although

ABOVE: Mickey Cave, who died tragically young, scored some memorable goals

BELOW: Colin Clarke (right) really took off at Bournemouth

ABOVE: Mark Newson (right) gets to grips with David Puckett at Craven Cottage as Cherries clinch promotion

BELOW: Eye on the ball . . .big striker Billy Rafferty

champions Bradford City were one of three sides on the receiving end of four-goal defeats during the Dean Court run-in. Manchester United gained revenge for the previous year's shock FA Cup defeat with a comfortable 3-0 win in the third round at Old Trafford.

During the summer Redknapp showed his eye for a bargain, picking up Colin Clarke from Tranmere for just £22,500, bringing Tommy Heffernan back from Sheffield United and signing Mark Newson from Maidstone. The season 1985/86 was another inconsistent campaign but Cherries proved their potential by beating runaway Division Three champions Reading home and away in the Milk Cup and also winning the League game at Elm Park. Everton were the opponents in the second round of the Milk Cup and goals by Clarke and Colin Russell (once Kenny Dalglish's understudy at Liverpool) saw Bournemouth go in 2-2 at half-time in the first leg at Goodison. Everton had Gary Lineker in attack but it was Heffernan's own goal in the second period which gave them a slender win, enhanced by a 2-0 victory in the second leg. Clarke starred for Northern Ireland in the 1986 World Cup in Mexico and made the short journey along the A38 to Southampton for a record-breaking £400,000. Striker David Puckett and defender Mark Whitlock moved the other way.

Redknapp also signed keeper Gerry Peyton, an Eire international, from Fulham, striker Carl Richards from non-league Enfield and midfield hard-man Tony Pulis from Newport County. With Ian Thompson forced to quit the professional game because of a pelvic injury Trevor Aylott was recruited from Chelsea for £15,000. This was the season when play-offs were introduced, giving the four clubs finishing below the top two the chance to fight it out for an additional promotion place. Had the system been around earlier it would have given Cherries several chances to go up. Now it was there, as things turned out, they wouldn't need it. Cherries started the season as 33/1 outsiders for the title. Skipper Newson conceded a penalty and scored a late equaliser in the opening game at Brentford. He would have a habit of notching crucial goals. Bristol City sent Bournemouth packing in the first round of the Littlewoods (formerly Milk and just plain League) Cup and

CLOCKWISE, FROM TOP LEFT: Harry Redknapp hoists the title trophy at Craven Cottage and congratulates Tony Sealy while Gerry Peyton, at home to Rotherham, has obviously put his shirt on going up

ABOVE: John Williams (left) and Tony Pulis salute fans at Fulham

BELOW: Harry Redknapp and Jimmy Gabriel raise a glass to promotion on the bus home

Orient did the same in the FA Cup second round - these early defeats were probably blessings in disguise as Redknapp could, to use the old cliche, concentrate on the League.

Cherries didn't lose in the League until their seventh game, at York, and made a habit of nicking games by the odd goal. They were also impressive away from home although there was the odd blip – Redknapp was manager of the month for October and on November 1 his side went down 4-0 at Middlesbrough. December brought successive defeats at home to Gillingham and away to Rotherham and it looked as though the old inconsistency would scupper another challenge. Then, on Boxing Day, John Williams, a big centre-half signed from Port Vale, scored in a confidence-boosting 3-0 win at Bristol Rovers. He was on the scoresheet again the following day as Fulham were beaten 3-2 at Dean Court. A new folk hero had arrived. Willo was to prove a key man. Six wins and four draws in the next 10 games, culminating in a 4-1 mauling of

Mansfield saw Cherries charge back to the top of the table with two goals apiece for Aylott and Richards. A setback at Bristol City was soon forgotten with a run of five straight wins including a blistering 3-1 demolition of nearest rivals Middlesbrough in front of almost 14,000 fans paying record receipts. Then another defeat at bogey side Gillingham was brushed aside with an unbeaten run of 11 games. During the run-in there were wins at Port Vale, Blackpool and Wigan, while Bournemouth were almost invincible at home. But promotion was confirmed in London with 4,000 supporters travelling up from the south coast to see Fulham swept aside 3-1, Peyton saving a penalty on his old stamping ground, Aylott scoring twice and Tony Sealy, on loan from Leicester, wrapping it up with a 25-yard piledriver in the closing minutes.

More than 11,000 fans packed Dean Court for the championship-deciding win over Rotherham, with Aylott and Richards the marksmen in a 2-0 win. Bournemouth's final total of 97 points surpassed the previous best, set by Oxford United in 1983/84. Three players were ever-present – Newson, Peyton and O'Driscoll – and the club notched up their 2,500th

ABOVE: Suits you sir ... Flash Harry meets fans at a civic reception at the Town Hall

BELOW: Big Willo ... always showed plenty of bottle

League game, against Bristol City in September. Pulis was the only outfield player not to score during the season.

ABOVE: From young fan to veteran newsman ... Colin Smith

MEMORIES – Colin Smith, who celebrated his 70th birthday in 1999, started watching Cherries as a child and reported on them for the Bournemouth Times and the Echo from the age of 21 until his retirement ...

'When I was a lad I used to love watching Jimmy Blair, Jack Kirkham and the rest. After I came out of the Army I joined the newspaper and a job came up on the sports desk. I was given a trial despite having no formal training and nearly 40 years later I was still doing it. I still haven't mastered shorthand. I had one spell away when I worked in Cambridgeshire for three years, so I missed the 1957 Cup run. The 1960s was a fairly dull time but the Bond era was brilliant and so was the promotion season under Harry. Plenty of managers came and went while I was covering the club – Bruton, Cox, McGarry, Welsh, Flewin, Benson, Hartley, Megson, Stock, Webb, Redknapp. I remember once giving Freddie Cox a lift to a night game at Shrewsbury in my Ford Anglia because he couldn't get away from his newsagents in Charminster in time to catch the team bus. I got on really well with Mickey Cave, Ted MacDougall and Harry. And Phil Boyer too, he was a lovely chap. I retired after we won the title in 1987 – I thought I'd get out at the top.'

ABOVE: Long-term sports editor at the Echo, Bob Harrison

Bob Harrison was sports editor at the Echo for 31 years from 1955 until he retired in 1986 ...

'I was friendly with some of the players in the early days. They were a great crowd. Tommy Godwin was a particular favourite of mine, and Ollie Norris too. They would wind each other up because they came from different parts of Ireland. Tommy would run out and chuck his false teeth in the back of the net with his cap and gloves, very funny. I laughed too when John King came down from Tranmere – he thought he was going to Brighton!'

CHAPTER 11

Takeover Turmoil

LEFT: Shaun Brooks (left) lit up midfield and harboured ambitions of playing for England

It should all have been hunky-dory, but, this being Bournemouth, it wasn't. The championship-clinching game against Rotherham had been preceded by the disruption of a cricket match on the adjacent Kings Park by a gang of bare-chested tattooed thugs. Although the vast majority of Bournemouth fans were, and always have been, generally well-behaved, there was a hard core of trouble-makers and the spectre of hooliganism still haunted the game The police insisted that the South and Brighton Beach ends should be fenced off and closed-circuit TV cameras installed for the coming season. This would cost the club £100,000 it could ill afford. Managing director Brian Tiler reluctantly decided to adopt a controversial membership scheme, similar to the one at Luton, which ruled out matchday ticket sales and would ultimately hit attendance figures. Another blow was the council's decision to reject plans to sell the ground and build a new £3m stadium at the nearby athletics track. Dean Court was showing signs of its age. And pre-season preparations were thrown into turmoil when chairman Rodney Barton's building firm went into receivership and he sold his 75 per cent controlling share to another builder, Birmingham-based Coventry fan Eric Grove. Barton, a keen yachtsman, stayed at the helm and the new owner said money would be available for new players. Redknapp was linked for the first time with the manager's job at his old club West Ham, where long-serving John Lyall was under threat, but his reward for taking Bournemouth higher than ever before was an improved three-year 'roll-over' contract. He celebrated by signing Shaun Brooks, a classy former Crystal Palace playmaker, for £10,000 from Orient. Meanwhile, Harry's son Jamie, 14, a pupil at Twynham in Christchurch, signed schoolboy forms for Spurs.

ABOVE: David Armstrong was forced to quit because of injury

Then, just weeks after the first takeover, cousins Geoffrey and Peter Hayward, the latter the son of Reg and grandson of Wilf, emerged from another £400,000 buy-out with a 60 per cent stake. Barton was replaced as chairman by another local businessman Jim Nolan, the second-largest shareholder, who immediately decided to put the new stadium on ice. Grove's company, Canberra, which may have bought the club for as little as £70,000 in the first deal, agreed to provide shirt sponsorship. The sale of land behind the Brighton Beach End for 26 houses, one of which was bought by goalkeeper Gerry Peyton, paid off a £600,000 bank loan but failed to show the expected profits, leaving the club £100,000 in debt following the championship season. David Armstrong, 32, joined on a free transfer from Southampton, and scored a hat-trick on his debut, a 4-4 draw with Spurs in a pre-season friendly. Another friendly, against Southampton, marked John Kirk's 25 years as trainer. Sadly, this game was marred by a pitch invasion by fighting fans which had to be broken up by police dogs. The fences went up soon after. After a turbulent close season it was a relief when the real action kicked off. Cherries won their first Division Two match, at Sheffield United, and beat Bradford City in their first home

77

game. They were among the early pace-setters, but already many fans didn't like the membership scheme and Redknapp didn't have the money he needed to buy a quality striker to convert the chances being created by Brooks and Armstrong. Nearly 10,500 saw Cherries beat Southampton 1-0 in the Littlewoods Cup second round first leg at Dean Court. Richard Cooke scored and big Willo had Colin Clarke in his pocket. Injury problems, especially up front, saw Bournemouth slide down the table after that promising start, but they drew 2-2 at The Dell in the second leg, O'Driscoll scoring the crucial goal to earn an aggregate victory, and were rewarded with a third round tie at Highbury which Arsenal cruised 3-0.

There was a long-running work permit wrangle over American striker Brent Goulet, who was soon shipped out on loan to Crewe. There were also more crowd control problems and a November break in Tenerife failed to lift the players, who went down at home to Huddersfield on their return. By contrast Manchester City, managed by Mel Machin, slammed 10 past Huddersfield and won 2-0 at Dean Court. Sections of the crowd started sniping at the players. A few months before they had been heroes, now they couldn't put a foot right. Redknapp's Christmas present was the promise of £100,000 to spend on a new striker. Two wins over the holiday period lifted Bournemouth up the table but they went out of the FA Cup, falling at the first hurdle at Brighton. Mark Newson returned from a long injury lay-off in February and was amazed to be one of several players barracked by the home crowd despite a 6-2 annihilation of Hull. The skipper called the boo boys 'disgraceful' while Redknapp pointed out, 'If our own supporters won't get behind us we've got no chance.' Armstrong returned as sub at Maine Road following a five-month absence but Machin's men, who had lost five home games on the trot, got back to winning ways and completed the double. Redknapp spent £70,000 of his Christmas windfall on Shaun Close from Spurs. The little front man scored some crucial goals as the tension mounted during a very tough run-in to the season. There were defeats at home to Aston Villa and away to Barnsley, where Armstrong, starting a match for the first time in six months, suffered a recurrence of the ankle injury

BELOW: American import Brent Goulet finally turned up

RIGHT: Hair-raising Ian Bishop only had one season at Bournemouth, but what a season!

which had dogged him throughout his brief and blighted Bournemouth career. Defeat at Blackburn left Cherries firmly anchored in the bottom three. They looked favourites to go down. The best they could hope for at this stage was to stay up through the play-offs. But Close scored his fourth goal in six games to clinch a surprise win at Ipswich and Bournemouth climbed three places. This was the game when Redknapp finally scrapped the sweeper system he had toyed with all season and reverted to a more conventional flat back four. A battling home draw with Leeds was followed by crushing defeats at Crystal Palace and relegation rivals Shrewsbury. Redknapp described Reading, just below Bournemouth in the table, as 'brutal' after the bruising goalless draw at Elm Park. Millwall won at Dean Court. It was looking grim, very grim. Then came three wins in seven days: Plymouth and Huddersfield away and Swindon at home. It had been a topsy-turvy, injury-hit, cash-strapped first season in Division Two, but Cherries had survived. Despite widespread complaints about the membership scheme (very popular with Prime Minister Margaret Thatcher) and the almost constant struggle against relegation, average gates had increased from 5,448 to 8,724. Nolan estimated relegation would have cost the club around £250,000. Paul Morrell was player of the year. He had been linked with a big-money move to Liverpool but decided to stay and signed a three-year deal. Williams, a Fulham target, did the same. And, before leaving for a pre-season tournament in Portugal, Redknapp picked up another staggering bargain, paying Carlisle just £35,000 at a transfer tribunal for ex-Everton midfielder Ian Bishop. Bradford City, who were prepared to pay £150,000, much closer to the asking price, couldn't get hold of the player after he had fallen into Redknapp's eager grasp. 'They couldn't get in touch,' said Harry enigmatically. 'They didn't know where he was.'

ABOVE: Striker Shaun Close joined from Tottenham

RIGHT: Paul Morrell (right) on an open-top bus tour of the town following the championship season with (from left) John Williams, Mark Whitlock, Carl Richards and Mark Newson

MEMORIES – Poole-born Paul Morrell missed just two games through suspension during the title-winning season. After giving up professional football he worked as a probation officer in Boscombe . . .

'When we won the title we weren't a great side but what we lacked in ability we more than made up for in team spirit. It was funny but we lost every pre-season friendly and didn't start the season that well. Then we just went on this incredible run after Christmas. We had people in the side like Willo and Mark Newson who were just born winners. It was so satisfying to finally bury the myth that we didn't want promotion. I was linked with Liverpool and Kenny Dalglish offered £300,000 for me but Harry turned it down – he used to call me Mister Consistency. I would like to have had the chance to play at Anfield, but it wasn't to be. Then later on Norwich and Chelsea came in for me but I stayed put. I look at the tight shorts we used to wear and doubt whether I could get them over one leg now, never mind two.'

Sheer Bliss

Wimbledon's shock FA Cup final victory over Liverpool in 1988 provoked an outspoken attack from Harry Redknapp. He said it was 'a black day for football. I won't let Bournemouth become another Wimbledon. I wouldn't have Vinnie Jones here for anything. He is a thug in football boots and sets a terrible example. He sickens me more than anything else in the game.' Redknapp promised his side would play entertaining football, and with Brooks and Bishop in his side it was an easy pledge to keep.

David Armstrong's ankle injury forced him to retire at 33. Former manager John Bond's son Kevin signed from Southampton for £50,000 and Redknapp restored the sweeper system to accommodate him. Young Luton striker Mark Stein was a target but he chose to sign for QPR for £300,000. His day at Dean Court would come. Cherries started the season as relegation favourites but once again got off to a flier. Little Richard Cooke even scored with a header to beat Chelsea and Brooks talked about hopefully playing for England. Mark Newson turned down a £200,000 move to Leicester because he believed Cherries would go up. A few games later he was dropped and when he was restored to the team the boo boys were on his back again. Crowds were disappointing and Redknapp said the atmosphere at home sometimes resembled a morgue. Then a flu epidemic ravaged the club as Coventry romped to a 7-1 aggregate victory in the Littlewoods Cup. Tony Pulis said the answer to the latest slump was hard work and he was promptly sent off as Cherries folded at home to Shrewsbury.

Mel Machin's Manchester City continued their dominance over Bournemouth, winning 1-0 at Dean Court with a goal by

ABOVE: Clap hands, here comes Kevin Bond, son of ex-boss John

RIGHT: Jumping for joy ... Luther Blissett found the Bournemouth air very much to his liking

a promising young striker called Paul Moulden. But Bournemouth's salvation was watching that game from the Main Stand. Luther Blissett was signed from Watford for £60,000. He had scored 168 goals for the Hornets, played 14 times for England and joined the elite £1m club with his move to AC Milan. He set himself a target of 12 before the end of the season after joining Cherries in November, then hit seven in his first four games including one on his debut in a 5-2 defeat at Barnsley and four in his first home game against Hull.

Colin Clarke returned on loan from Southampton and scored on his comeback just minutes after trotting on as sub, then set up the winner for Blissett. The crowd of 8,000-plus was 3,000 up on the previous game. Goalscorers have always attracted big crowds at Bournemouth There was Eyre in the 20s and 30s, McGibbon in the 40s, Newsham in the 50s and no-one much after Dowsett's departure in the early 60s until MacDougall and Clarke briefly lit up the 70s. The goals had been shared around in the 80s between players like Morgan, Thompson, Aylott, Richards, Funnell and Puckett. But the real sensation, the man who got the crowd buzzing again, was Blissett.

He'd been cruelly dubbed Luther Miss-it during his unsuccessful spell in defence-dominated Italy but he could barely put a foot wrong in the less-pressured surroundings of Dorset. His ninth goal in eight games in a 2-1 home win over Brighton put Bournemouth in the play-off places in the New Year and the FA Cup was shaping up nicely with wins over Blackpool and Hartlepool earning a dream home tie against Manchester United, now managed by Alex Ferguson, in round five.

Redknapp signed defender Shaun Teale for £50,000 from his old mate Stuart Morgan at Weymouth. Morgan followed soon after as chief scout. Young left-sided utility man David Coleman scored the winner as Cherries beat West Brom in front of a huge crowd in search of ticket vouchers for the United showdown and Scandinavian advertisers boosted the Dean Court coffers by £50,000 as the big match was being shown live on TV in Norway, Sweden and Denmark. Queues started to form at 2am on the day the United tickets went on sale. The match ended 1-1 with Aylott cancelling out Mark Hughes' opener. Blissett had a strong penalty appeal turned down and Ferguson

TOP: Pointing the way . . . bargain buy Shaun Teale

ABOVE: Promising David Coleman, like Arnold Stephens, Alan Groves and Mickey Cave, was another player whose life was cut tragically short

ABOVE: This Cookie didn't crumble ... flying winger Richard Cooke was a key man

admitted, 'We deserved to lose.' Russell Beardsmore, later to move to Dean Court, was on the bench for the visitors. O'Driscoll's under-hit back-pass gifted Brian McClair the only goal in the replay. A £60,000 windfall was Cherries' consolation.

They continued to do well in the League, winning 3-2 at Crystal Palace, whose manager Steve Coppell said, 'They were the whipping boys last season, now they're born-again.' Redknapp, a keen gambler, took an £18,000 punt on another non-league player, Cheltenham's Peter Shearer, in an effort to clinch a play-off place. Cherries climbed to fifth with a 3-0 win over Bradford City and the outspoken Redknapp again hit out at the 'miserable' crowds. 'I'm not having a go at our regular supporters, they're greatly appreciated,' he said. 'But where are all those people who were clamouring for tickets for the United game and complaining how disgraceful it was we didn't have a bigger ground?' The stayaway fans hit back, complaining of poor facilities and long queues at the turnstiles. Tiler admitted he had blundered by adding £1 to ticket prices to raise money for the Clapham rail disaster fund. Another tragedy, at Hillsborough where 96 Liverpool fans were crushed to death, prompted calls for the fences to come down. Cherries slumped out of contention, but what had happened at Clapham and Sheffield put events on the pitch into stark perspective. Younger players like Coleman and Matty Holmes were given a run and Nolan spoke of a 'super safe' new stadium near Hurn Airport as Redknapp labelled Dean Court 'an embarrassment.' Liverpool's Kenny Dalglish joined a growing list of managers keen on Bishop. He saw the midfielder sparkle as Cherries pulled back a three-goal half-time deficit at Manchester City to equalise with a penalty by Blissett in injury-time in a thrilling fightback. Moulden scored twice for City, who were promoted, and Redknapp logged the name in his memory bank.

Plymouth fans caused havoc at Cherries' last home game of the season. Final position, 12th, was a big improvement. Blissett, with 21 goals in 35 games, was player of the season. Bishop, who signed a new four-year deal, wasn't far behind. John Lyall was sacked at Upton Park and Redknapp, the favourite to succeed him, was disappointed that Nolan refused him permission to speak to West Ham. Bishop got the Division One stage

LEFT: 'I'm on your side mate' . . . Paul Moulden (left) and Gavin Peacock battle for possession

BELOW: Mark Newson captained Cherries to title but still took stick from the supporters

his sublime talents deserved, signing for Manchester City in a £725,000 deal which saw Moulden, who made the Guiness Book of Records as a schoolboy with more than 200 goals in a single season, move the other way. Other new signings included attacking midfielder Gavin Peacock and keeper Phil Kite, from Gillingham, with Pulis heading back up to Kent. Season ticket sales soared and Jamie Redknapp, 16, joined up with his dad and older brother Mark, a defender, at Dean Court very much against the wishes of his former Spurs boss Terry Venables.

Jim Nolan switched his attention for a new stadium site from Hurn to Poole as the capacity at Dean Court was cut to just over 11,000 for safety reasons. Redknapp took his summer spending up to £580,000 by signing ex-Saints winger George Lawrence from Millwall and ex-Spurs defender Paul Miller from Watford. Early in the season Hull revisited the scene of their 5-1 destruction a year before. It won't be so easy this time, warned Redknapp, and he was right. Cherries once again scored five,

ABOVE: Young Jamie Redknapp brushes up on his football skills

ABOVE RIGHT: New boys . . . (left to right) Gavin Peacock, George Lawrence, Paul Miller, Phil Kite and Paul Moulden

but they also conceded four. This time Luther scored just once while Moulden got a hat-trick and followed up with a couple more in the win over Newcastle. A maddeningly inconsistent season followed with several players suffering from long-term injuries. Teale, Holmes, Coleman and Peacock did well while Moulden was great at home but struggled to score away.

An ex-soldier called Guy Whittingham, the subject of a failed bid by Bournemouth the previous season, scored the only goal as Portsmouth visited Dean Court in the League. Former skipper Fred Marsden died in November 1989, the same month that Newson was stripped of the captaincy and put on the transfer list following a touchline bust-up with his manager at Bradford. Bond took over the armband. But yet another injury crisis meant Newson was soon back in the fold while the consistent O'Driscoll continued to rack up the games on his way to a record number of appearances. Redknapp and Tiler both faced FA disrepute charges for getting lippy with refs and young Jamie came into the picture following the popular Mark 'Dessie' O'Connor's move to Gillingham. Peyton saved two penalties yet Cherries still crashed out of the FA Cup at Sheffield United. Government scientists said seaside scents wafted into packed football grounds would reduce hooliganism, but the Dorset police football liaison officer preferred to stick with the tried and trusted CCTV and membership schemes.

In January 1990 Harry Redknapp became the club's longest serving manager at six years three months and, with over half the season gone, Blissett steered Cherries to a comfortable mid-table position with a hat-trick against Ipswich. The Taylor Report into the Hillsborough disaster recommended all-seater stadiums for clubs in the top two divisions. World Cup stars Gheorghe Hagi, Marius Lacatus and the rest of star-studded Steaua Bucharest line-up played a friendly at Dean Court. Lou Macari quit at West Ham and Harry Redknapp was again linked with the job, but it went to Billy Bonds.

Newson moved to Fulham and soon afterwards another clutch of injuries meant striker Denny Mundee and teenager Paul Mitchell had to step in at a crucial stage. Teale, previously a rock at the back, was ruled out for the rest of the season. Moulden was sold and Chelsea turned down an approach for Graham Roberts. Slowly but surely Cherries were being sucked into the relegation dogfight. Jamie Redknapp played his first full game at West Ham where Ian Bishop had ended up after his spell at Maine Road. 'He (Bishop) was telling me to keep going and encouraging me all the time,' said a thankful Jamie.

Plymouth won a six-pointer at Dean Court to send Bournemouth into the bottom three for the first time. Blissett missed a penalty in the home defeat against Leicester and a disgusted O'Driscoll hit out at the South End fans who chanted Moulden's name during the game. An angry mob threw coins at the sponsors lounge and chanted 'Sack the board.' Things were turning very ugly. Nolan asked 'What crisis?' and Redknapp defended his transfer record. Machin was now at Barnsley where Cherries won 1-0 to give themselves a glimmer of hope. Everything rested on the final game, at home to Leeds United.

ABOVE: Romanian superstar Gheorge Hagi came to Dean Court with Steaua Bucharest

BELOW: First test for 1988-89, facing the cameras

RIGHT: Matty Holmes hitches a
lift from Luther Blissett

MEMORIES – Luther Blissett turned down Harry Redknapp's offer of a
year's contract in 1991 and eventually returned to his first club,
Watford. He said at the time . . .
'I've looked after myself and that has given me the chance to play until
I'm 35. There are far more gifted players than me, I'm the first to admit
that, but not many have got as much out of the game as I have. I was
unhappy with my Bournemouth home debut against Hull – I scored
four but I should have had six.' (Redknapp said, 'He has been a magnificent buy for this club, on and off the pitch. He's super-fit. His body is so
good I'd like to borrow it one day.')

Rioting and Roman Tragedy

The writing was on the wall in more ways than one. Leeds needed a win to clinch the title. Cherries needed a win to stay up (they also needed other results to go their way.) But it was a May Bank Holiday weekend and the Yorkshire club had a notorious following. Bournemouth, the town not the football club, needed this game about as much as an oil spill on the beach. Leeds' allocation of 2,800 tickets had long since been sold. Elland Road officials planned to screen the match live at six venues in the city to try and prevent fans without tickets travelling down. Dorset police, who had been told something unpleasant was afoot, were on red alert.

Vinnie Jones, then at Leeds, vilified by Harry Redknapp a couple of years before, issued a public appeal to the club's supporters, 'Enjoy yourself and the game but leave out the aggro.' Fat

RIGHT: A riot policeman faces up to Leeds fans in Kings Park

LEFT: AFC Bournemouth 1990-91 (back, l to r) George Lawrence, Denny Mundee, Matty Holmes, Shaun Teale, Paul Mitchell, Paul Miller, Peter Shearer; (middle) Terry Shanahan, Efan Ekoku, Jamie Redknapp, Peter Guthrie, Trevor Aylott, John Williams, Paul Morrell, Stuart Morgan, Tony Pulis; (front) John Kirk, Luther Blissett, Sean O'Driscoll, Kevin Bond, Gavin Peacock, David Coleman and John Dickens

chance. Leeds fans wearing 'Bournemouth Invasion 90' T-shirts started rolling into town in the days leading up to the game. They rampaged through the streets smashing shop windows, starting fires and fighting running battles with riot police. Mounted police from London were drafted in. As many as 6,000 Leeds fans were estimated to have descended on Bournemouth, many with forged tickets bought back home. Shops were looted and hotel guests kept awake by sirens. Almost 100 people were arrested and 30 injured in the rioting. Holidaymakers near the pier were hit by a barrage of stones, women were indecently assaulted and a 12-year-old boy attacked for daring to wear an AFC Bournemouth shirt. A police inspector was severely concussed after being hit on the head by a lump of concrete as 700 police in riot gear prevented the ticketless Leeds fans from getting into the ground. The senior officer was convinced that if they had got in, 'we would have had another Hillsborough on our hands.' Cricket and bowls matches at Kings Park had been relocated or postponed as matchday trouble was not just expected but inevitable. But no-one could have guessed just how bad it would be.

ABOVE: Peter Shearer (right) tangles with Leeds' Lee Chapman

Leeds fans who had bought Main Stand tickets on the black market intimidated Cherries chief scout Stuart Morgan and home supporters. Defender Paul Miller said it was the worst day of his 15-year career. 'They are just scum. I feared for our supporters.' Two Leeds fans had jumped into the player's car, which was being driven by his wife, on the way to the game and almost caused a serious accident as she tried to escape. Missiles, including rocks, were thrown at the pitch. Children were in tears. Home supporters who had turned up hoping to cheer their side to safety forgot about the football and feared for their lives instead. Bournemouth's players were clearly unnerved. That's not a biased excuse, it's a fact. The Echo's David Edwards said the hooligan element attached to Leeds was like 'a lingering, malicious disease . . . the game seemed almost immaterial in the light of violence in the town and the air of menace which hung around Dean Court, normally one of football's most tranquil arenas.' On the pitch, a single goal, scored by Lee Chapman in the 49th minute, was enough to clinch the title for Leeds and end Cherries' three-year stay in the Second Division.

The Home Office asked Football League chiefs to explain

why they had ignored police advice to bring the game forward. Bournemouth briefly held out hope that scandal-ridden Swindon, accused of making irregular payments to players, would be relegated in their stead, but it was not to be. The football club's critics in Bournemouth had a field day as the riot fall-out rumbled on. Even the MP got involved. There was a growing call for the Cherries and their associated problems to be booted out of town. There had been some bad times at Dean Court, but there was never anything to compare with this.

Normal service was resumed after the heady flirtation with Division Two and the horror of the Battle of Bournemouth. As Cherries went down ticket prices went up. The club was £600,000 in debt and losing £10,000 a week. The players remained on high inflation-proof wages and police costs were up as understandable paranoia set in. Redknapp once again tried to prise Graham Roberts away from Chelsea and brought in a lightning-quick striker called Efan Ekoku from non-league Sutton United. Brian Tiler resigned after seven years as managing director, saying he had been unhappy for a while and had not been looking forward to returning from the end-of-season tour of the USA. 'My job was very much about motivation. If I could not motivate myself there was no chance I could motivate others.' Nolan said, 'He has done a marvellous job for this club. How can we replace him?' then answered his own question by saying there would be no replacement. The Football League fudged the convoluted Swindon scandal. The Wiltshire club had won promotion from Division Two with illegally-signed players. They were demoted to Three and Tranmere went up to Two instead of Bournemouth remaining there, as precedent surely demanded. Respected football writer Patrick Barclay, in the Independent, called it 'a senseless and staggering blunder.' That decision probably cost Cherries between £300,000 and £400,000 in lost revenue from sponsorship and gate receipts. Nolan said, 'You don't get anything in this world for finishing second, but Tranmere have.' Kevin Bond was realistic: 'At the end of the day we just weren't good enough to stay in the Second.' Cherries wanted to take the League to court but were dissuaded by potential legal costs of up to £400,000, and hoteliers spoke of suing the League for compensation for damage and cancelled bookings due to the Leeds riot. Assistant manager Jimmy Gabriel returned to Everton, saying the offer to work alongside Colin Harvey at Goodison was too good to turn down, and Redknapp and Tiler set off to Italy to watch the World Cup. The two men were in a mini-bus with officials from other English clubs returning to their hotels in the early hours after watching a match involving the the host nation. The mini-bus was in collision with a sports car containing three young Italian fans on the Rome-Naples road near the town of Latina. Tiler, 47, was killed and so were the three in the car, which had crossed to the wrong side of the road. Redknapp was dragged unconscious and covered in petrol from the wreckage by Michael Sinclair, the chairman of York City. Redknapp didn't come round for two days. He said, 'We had stopped for a pizza and to avoid the traffic. I remember thinking we were almost home and then I must have dropped off. Brian was a wonderful warm bloke, a very close friend.' Redknapp suffered serious injuries including a fractured skull, broken nose, cracked ribs and a deep gash in his left leg.

ABOVE: Harry Redknapp recovers with a hug from wife Sandra

An FA board of appeal overturned the League's decision to demote Swindon to the Third Division and put them in the Second instead. So Tranmere were dumped back into the Third with Cherries. Nolan, understandably, said, 'It's a joke. The whole thing has been a farce.' Stuart Morgan acted as caretaker manager while Redknapp recovered at a private hospital in Bournemouth. Pulis returned from Gillingham as player-coach with Terry Shanahan becoming assistant manager. The board finally gave in to fan power and dropped the controversial membership scheme. On the field it was the same old story of inconsistency and injuries. Peter Shearer, on the verge of a £500,000 move to Wimbledon, was badly injured in a horrifying collision with Bradford City goalkeeper Paul Tomlinson and would never fully regain the fitness and inspirational form he had shown in the early part of that season. The players had been promised a share of £200,000 if they went up. Redknapp returned to work in mid-October, still suffering severe headaches, with no sense of smell or taste. But his appetite for football was undiminished.

RIGHT: Peter Shearer in agony
after being injured against
Bradford City at Dean Court

MEMORIES – Duncan Lee, chief photographer at the Daily Echo, was
on duty over the weekend when rioting rocked Bournemouth . . .
'I have never seen anything like it – never been so frightened – in my
20 years as a newspaper photographer. I was punched, spat at and
threatened by Leeds fans, both in the town the night before and at the
game itself. Somebody threw a brick at me which missed my head by
inches and shattered the lens of the camera I was holding to my face.
The police were advancing on the Leeds fans, banging their sticks
against their shields. I tried to take a breather behind the police cordon
but they threw me back at the mercy of the mob. They said "If you're
not one of us, you're one of them." It was absolutely terrifying,'

CHAPTER
14

Nearly Men

Efan Ekoku, born in Manchester, raised in Liverpool, eligible for Nigeria, welcomed Redknapp back with his first League goal in a stirring 3-0 home win over Fulham. Birmingham boss Dave Mackay finally signed Trevor Aylott after a 14-month pursuit of the big target man, an unsung hero who had served Bournemouth well. Welsh international Andy Jones arrived from Charlton for £80,000 and scored with a blistering shot just 74 seconds into his home debut against Tranmere. John Bond returned to Dean Court as a manager for the first time since his acrimonious departure in 1973 and saw his Shrewsbury side beaten 3-2 with Gavin Peacock scoring a sensational overhead goal. Jim Nolan resigned as chairman 'to spend more time with

LEFT: Speed merchant . . . Efan Ekoku in full flow on his way to a goal against Shrewsbury

RIGHT: Peter Hayward carried on the family tradition

ABOVE: The line-up for 1991/92 ..
(back, l to r) Jones, Lawrence,
Mundee, O'Driscoll, Fereday,
Morrell; (middle) Kirk, Bond,
Morris, Watson, Bartram,
Williams, Quinn, Ekoku, Coleman,
Hardwick; (front) Pulis, Baker,
Holmes, Rowland, Redknapp,
Case, Cooke, Brooks, Shanahan

his family and on his business' and was replaced by Peter Hayward, a former Football League referee and a director for 20 years. Hayward was following in the footsteps of his grandfather, father and uncle. He said, 'The first thing I must do is get the finances sorted out.' Poole Stadium owner Derek Block said he was interested in taking over and moving Cherries to Poole. Redknapp threatened to quit if that happened.

Cherries' 100th FA Cup victory, over Gillingham at Dean Court, earned them a home tie with Hayes, who were beaten 1-0 (Brooks in the 88th minute.) The unsettled Gavin Peacock joined Newcastle with Bournemouth getting winger Wayne Fereday and £150,000 in return. A 5-0 hammering at Grimsby provoked Redknapp into a stinging rebuke. 'We were a disgrace,' he said. 'There are a few players struggling to justify their future. They are getting good money, they had better start earning it.' Jamie Redknapp, just 17, joined Kenny Dalglish at Liverpool for £350,000, a record fee for a teenager, having started just six League games for Cherries. Anfield stopper Alex Watson came to Bournemouth for £100,000 and the annual meeting revealed losses of almost £850,000 for the year and an overdraft of £1.5m. Chairman Hayward said the wage bill had gone up by £500,000, income had fallen by £200,000 and bank interest charges were up £90,000. The club had set an unwel-

ABOVE AND TOP RIGHT: Fans'
favourite Paul Wood pictured in
spectacular action

RIGHT: Andy Jones celebrates his
goal just 74 seconds into his
home debut against Tranmere

ABOVE AND RIGHT: Old hands
Jimmy Case and Jimmy Quinn provided, respectively, guile in
midfield and goals up front

come record. Four-thousand fans made the short journey to
Fratton Park for the FA Cup fourth round where the pace of
Pompey's Guy Whittingham brought him four goals in a 5-1
rout. Back in the League Bournemouth were handily-placed but
Blissett kept missing from the penalty spot at vital times. A Jones
double against Reading steered his side into a play-off spot.
Blissett reached 50 League goals from 102 appearances and
Richard Cooke returned on a free from Luton via Spurs to score
some vital goals. Redknapp spoke optimistically of automatic pro-
motion. Then old boy John Beck's Cambridge United won at
Dean Court with their route one stuff, not pretty but effective,
and overpowered Bournemouth again at the Abbey Stadium.

Again it went right down to the wire. Again Cherries were crushed in the sun, this time at John Bond's Shrewsbury. Coach Pulis said, 'We're the nearly men, not good enough,' and the manager blamed Teale, twice player of the year, for two of the goals in a 3-1 defeat. But it was in midfield where most of the damage was done by Shrews' Tony 'The Belly' Kelly. Two thousand travelling fans were well and truly gutted.

The overdraft was now up to £2m and all the players were available for sale. Pulis was touted as Gerry Francis's replacement at Bristol Rovers while Redknapp thought long and hard about joining Stoke. He was also the 'people's choice' to take over from Chris Nicholl at Southampton. Blissett, with 56 goals from 121 games, went back to Watford, Peyton joined up again with Gabriel at Everton and Teale moved to Aston Villa for £300,000. Peter Hayward resigned on health grounds and Colin Legg became the third chairman in eight months. The South End fences, unpopular with the fans, came down. Jimmy Case, 37-year-old ex-Liverpool legend, goalkeeper Vince Bartram, central defender Mark Morris and striker Jimmy Quinn gave the new-look side an experienced spine. Case was

ABOVE: Cherries' first woman chief executive Annie Bassett

LEFT: The man with the headband ...injury forced Trevor Aylott to adopt some unusual headwear

BELOW: Ian Botham (right) joins Cherries for training during the pantomime season

ABOVE: Fog on the Tyne ... Jimmy Case muses over the FA Cup postponement at Newcastle

made captain, taking over from Kevin Bond who would suffer stick from the fans but show great character to come back from injury and win them over again to pick up the player of the season award. The mixture of grizzled veterans and promising youngsters like Keith Rowland, Matty Holmes and Denny Mundee took time to gel. The directors had to put together a rescue package after the bank became nervous over the council's decree that Dean Court could not be sold for housing. Purbeck-based scrap dealer Norman Hayward, 52, a former Cherries reserve team player, bought the 61 per cent controlling stake and deposited £500,000 with the bank to reduce the overdraft. Director Ken Gardiner put up £40,000 to buy fans' favourite Paul Wood following the winger's fourth stay on loan. The debts mounted to almost £2.7m and, with Christmas looming, family man Redknapp revealed he hadn't been paid since the start of the season. Norman Hayward appealed for £250,000 from local businesses and warned the club could be days from closure. A lottery scheme, Cherry Aid, was launched and individual supporters were asked to form racehorsing-style syndicates to buy players and gamble on a share of any profits. A near-capacity crowd, the biggest for two years, showed up for the FA Cup third round game with Newcastle and listened in silence as Redknapp urged them to chip in. 'If we all pull together we can save this club,' said Harry. He was to be proved right, but not straight away. More than 100 supporters travelled to St James's Park for the Newcastle replay only for the fog which blighted their 18-hour return trip to cause the game to be abandoned after just 17 minutes. The replayed replay was screened on Sky, the Cherries' first appearance on live TV. Gavin Peacock gave the Geordies the lead against his old club, Wood equalised. The home team went ahead in extra-time only for Bond to calmly draw Cherries level and send the game into a penalty shoot-out, only the second in the history of the FA Cup. Quinn, Mundee, Cooke and Brooks all kept their cool to score from the spot while Liam O'Brien blazed his shot over the bar and Vince Bartram saved from Kevin Brock. 'We practised penalties in training,' revealed Bartram afterwards. 'And I didn't stop one.' The game earned Cherries a much-needed £40,000 in gate receipts and TV money. There was light at the end of the tunnel although Bournemouth lost in the next round at Ipswich and missed out on a dream tie with Liverpool.

ABOVE: Penalty king . . . Vince Bartram was the shot-stopping hero at St James's Park

Trainer John Kirk announced his retirement after 30 years and Ekoku shrugged off his injury worries to appear in the sprint challenge before the Rumbelows (ex-League, ex-Milk, ex-Littlewoods) Cup final at Wembley. He didn't win the race but he returned refreshed to score twice as Swansea went down 3-0 at Dean Court and Cherries moved into play-off contention. Annie Bassett struck a blow for womankind, taking over from Brian Wells as chief executive. Neighbouring non-league Wimborne Town won the FA Vase at Wembley on the same day that Quinn scored from the spot with the last kick of the game to clinch three points against Reading and keep promotion hopes alive. There were all sorts of possible permutations as Bournemouth went into their last game of the 1991/92 season at Hartlepool, but for the third successive year it all went pear-shaped. A 1-0 defeat meant another season that had promised so much had ended in massive disappointment.

ABOVE: John 'Captain' Kirk in the Dean Court boot room

MEMORIES – John Kirk, former Bolton and Poole goalkeeper, spent 30 years as trainer at Dean Court before retiring in 1991 ...

'I worked under a dozen different managers and I liked them all. They had one thing in common – they expected the players to be able to do what they were able to do as players themselves, and the things they couldn't do! Brian Tiler offered me a job for life. I did all sorts of jobs – I was in charge of the reserve side, scout, physio, trainer, kitman. Everything but manager, I wasn't that daft! My wife Phyllis would help me darn the socks and sew numbers on the shirts. It was John Bond's wife Janet who pointed out that I looked and sounded like Tommy Cooper. I bought a fez on a tour of Turkey and used to do impressions to cheer up the players. I also did John Arlott, the cricket commentator. The Bond era was the best time for me, the championship season a close second. I was good friends with Stan Newsham and Harry Hughes, but the old trainer Arthur Cunliffe advised me not to get too close to the players. It was Phil Holder who gave me the nickname Captain, after a horse in the Grand National, not the Star Trek character.'

CHAPTER
15

Harrygate

Harry Redknapp, after nine roller-coaster years at the club, was the League's fourth longest-serving manager. He had 12 players out of contract and wasn't relishing another rebuilding job. He had turned down several chances to join bigger clubs on bigger money. But it still came as a shock when he resigned in June 1992, saying, 'I need a change and a new challenge. I am also convinced that the club will benefit by having a fresh face. This is purely a personal decision and I must stress there is no question of any other issue forcing me into this situation. The

LEFT: Harry Redknapp looks glum as he considers his resignation

TOP: Calling for commitment . . .
new manager Tony Pulis

ABOVE: Pulis's assistant David
Williams even played a few games
in midfield for Cherries

important thing for me now is to have a complete break from football.' Less than a month later Redknapp was back at Upton Park as assistant to his good friend Billy Bonds.

Coach Tony Pulis took the Bournemouth manager's job with Redknapp's blessing. The directors contacted him in Florida where he was on holiday with his family. The family's return journey was a nightmare, the plane was hit by lightning, fortunately while it was still on the runway. When Pulis eventually got back to Bournemouth he said he must have been 'daft' to replace the most popular manager ever at the club and immediately demanded total commitment. He also took Cherries straight into Division Two, but only because the old Division One was now called the Premiership. Chairman Norman Hayward said the new man wasn't a cheap option. 'Harry's opinion was a major influence. It was important that Tony agreed we should be looking to continue to play good football.' Pulis himself ruled out 'route one' and said Cherries wouldn't play the Cambridge way. He also booted out Redknapp's backroom team with Terry Shanahan and Stuart Morgan making way for David Williams, a former teammate at Bristol Rovers. Jimmy Quinn was sold to Reading, where he would continue to bang in the goals, and replaced by Steve Fletcher a gangling 19-year-old centre-forward from Hartlepool. 'Be patient,' Pulis urged supporters. 'He's not the finished article but he has real potential.'

West Ham made a pre-season friendly visit in August with Ian Bishop and a new coach, one Harry Redknapp, in their ranks. Redknapp got a standing ovation from the home fans and a statuette of a racehorse from Norman Hayward. Stewards took charge of security inside the ground to cut back on police costs and everyone at Dean Court was looking forward to the new season. But the Redknapp resignation story would run and run. It became known as 'Harrygate'. The accounts were made public just before Christmas and revealed that Redknapp had been given a £100,000 'golden handshake' when he quit, on the understanding that he was taking a break from the game. This pay-out infuriated some supporters who threatened to boycott Cherry Aid in protest. Even the council got in on the act, witholding a £15,000 grant for car park improvements. Hayward tried to defuse the controversy by saying the money had come from his own pocket. 'The payment has not, and will not, cost the club a penny,' he said. If the board had known Redknapp was going to another job so soon after leaving Bournemouth the money would probably not have been paid.

Redknapp continued to claim he did not have a job lined up when he left Dean Court, saying, 'My conscience is completely and utterly clear.' He had signed a three-year roll-over contract and it would have cost the club over £200,000 to sack him. He said he no longer felt welcome at Dean Court at the time he quit. 'Certain things had happened and I could no longer work with certain people.' He said he had told the board he would not hold them to ransom over his contract and the agreed deal was fair to both sides. It would later emerge in Redknapp's book that he had clashed with director Ken Gardiner who had publicly embarrassed Kevin Bond at a post-match presentation.

Norman Hayward had spent 30 years with non-league Swanage Town as player and official before offering to help out at Dean Court. The change in surroundings was drastic and devastating for him. On several occasions during the forthcoming season he was forced to pay the players' wages himself. On more than one occasion he drove to the ground with wads of notes stashed in plastic supermarket carrier bags. The Echo commented, 'The game off the field seems no less prone to switches of tactics, runs down the wing, trips in the penalty area and disastrous own goals. No doubt over the years the Cherries-Redknapp saga will gather all the apocryphal moss that attaches to folklore. It is a good story but actually not as important as another annual general meeting revelation – the fact that Cherries directors injected £400,000 into the club last year to improve the financial situation. The move shows spectacular commitment. Since the next goal is more important than the last, THIS is the magnanimous gesture the supporters should applaud and remember.'

RIGHT: Harry Redknapp returns with West Ham and receives a statuette from Norman Hayward

MEMORIES - Harry Redknapp, who served AFC Bournemouth as player, coach and manager . . .

'I have some great memories. Being manager of the first side to reach the Second (now First) Division was the best time for me, especially as there had been all sorts of silly rumours going round town that we didn't want to go up, or couldn't afford to. And to win the title as well, with 97 points, now that was special. That was such a great set of lads – Willo, Sean O'Driscoll, big Trevor Aylott, Cookie, Dessie O'Connor, Mark Newson and the rest. I picked up some real bargains while I was at Dean Court, people like Shaun Teale, Ian Bishop and Colin Clarke. When I wanted to sign Clarkie for 25 grand the board said we couldn't afford him, so I got together a group of local businessmen who were prepared to stump up the cash. When the directors realised how serious we were they changed their minds and came up with the money. The worst time was Brian Tiler's death. When he arrived the club was going nowhere and the crowds were poor. He gave the whole place such a lift from day one. Of course, I still have a place in my heart for Bournemouth. I went through so much there. I always look out for their results and I want them to do well, unless they're playing West Ham, of course!'

Purple Reign

Steve Fletcher, Adrian Pennock and teenager Scott Mean made their debuts at Preston where a new-look Cherries line-up trotted out in a new-look strip – a garish, predominantly purple outfit. (The home kit, mainly green, was little better.) Another interesting innovation for 1992/93 was the Echo's introduction of marks out of 10 for the players, some of whom have been known to accost a reporter if they feel they've been hard done by. (Mean was the first star man, getting top marks with seven out of 10.) Keith Rowland, 21, was called up by Northern Ireland and Matty Holmes went to West Ham for a mere £40,000, but beggars can't be choosers. Bournemouth, although hard to beat, weren't winning many games either. Goals were hard to come by and crowds were down. Injuries

LEFT: Scott Mean was voted the Echo's first star man after the paper introduced marks out of 10

ABOVE: Muddy marvel ... Denny Mundee slides in to score in the FA Cup replay at Barnet

continued to pile up. Physio Steve Hardwick, who served aboard hospital ship Canberra during the Falklands conflict, said the treatment room was like a war zone– with Shearer, Wood and Ekoku out long-term. Stoke's Mark Stein scored twice as Bournemouth slid inexorably down the table. Pulis and Shaun Brooks, who had been out injured since the start of the season, had a 'disagreement' outside the dressing-room which left the midfielder reportedly needing stitches to his face. Brooks wasn't speaking to anyone about the incident, apart from the PFA, the players' union, while Pulis merely said, 'It's a man's game. Maybe he hit himself on a door or something after I had gone.'

During the dour goalless FA Cup draw with Barnet the ground was rife with speculation that Pulis would soon be off to Bristol Rovers to be replaced by John Beck, whose Cambridge were about as entertaining to watch as back-to-back episodes of Beadle's About. Talk about frying pan and fire! Bournemouth-born teenager Christer Warren scored Cheltenham's goal in a 1-1 draw at Whaddon Road in the next round of the Cup. Cherries won the replay 3-0 to earn a third-round tie at Blackburn, the big-money side of the moment. Pulis called in Jack Mitchell, a sports psychologist to help prepare the team. Pennock said, 'Jack told us Rovers were nothing special and we would beat them.' Mitchell was only half-right – the first half, when Cherries led through Ekoku's goal – but Rovers, even without Alan Shearer, stepped up a gear after the break to win.

Full-back Neil Masters, nicknamed 'Rhino' because he was built like one, blasted his way into the lead in a magazine competition to find the man with the hardest shot in the game. His hammer-like left foot launched the ball at 85mph – but England's Stuart 'Psycho' Pearce was still waiting to have his go. Keith Rowland, Masters' friend and rival for the left-back spot, had been sent to Coventry, on trial. Pulis admitted there had been another 'disagreement' between himself and the stylish young defender, 'but nothing that isn't part and parcel of football.' The smallest crowd to see a competitive first team match at Dean Court since 1923, a mere 1,218, watched the Autoglass Trophy (which began life as the Associate Members Cup) game against Reading. On-loan Dave Smith was injured warming up so sub Rob Murray, 18, stepped off the bench to score twice on his full debut, a 5-1 win over Blackpool. Another sub, Sean O'Driscoll, remained in the dug-out clutching a silver plate after breaking Ray Bumstead's appearances record.

BELOW: Squad for 1993/94 . . . (back, left to right) Mike Trusson, Adrian Pennock, Steve Fletcher, Mark Morris, Alex Watson, Peter Shearer, Stuart Kerr, John Williams; (middle) Mike McElhatton, Keith Rowland, Joe Parkinson, Vince Bartram, Neil Moss, Neil Masters, Rob Murray, David Williams; (front) Steve Hardwick, Mark O'Connor, Paul Wood, Russell Beardsmore, Tony Pulis, Scott Mean, Brian McGorry, Paul Mitchell, Sean O'Driscoll

With Ekoku leading the way Bournemouth suddenly found their scoring touch and started climbing up the table. Superb goalkeeping by Bartram and a brilliant individual goal by Wood earned a great win at Rotherham. Premiership scouts were flocking to Dean Court and Pulis was manager of the month for February. Norwich snapped up Ekoku in a record-breaking £750,000 deal on the stroke of the transfer deadline. It was an offer that hard-up Cherries couldn't refuse although the trading loss for the year had been halved in the face of a deep recession. A knee injury forced Richard Cooke to retire at just 27. His old teammates slipped back, perilously close to the relegation places, and some fans were critical of the style of play. Safety was secured in the penultimate game at Stockport which aptly finished goalless. It had been the club's worst season for nine years with just 45 goals in 46 League games and only 12 victories. The players went on tour to Africa to get over it and Pulis said, 'The directors made it clear that survival was the name of the game. Frankly it was never going to be pretty.'

Joe Parkinson, Russell Beardsmore, Steve Cotterill, Chris Leadbitter and old boy Mark O'Connor were drafted in for 1993/94. Rowland and Poole-born Paul Mitchell linked up

TOP: Steve Cotterill salutes another goal

ABOVE: Midfield maestro Joe Parkinson joined Everton

RIGHT: Mark O'Connor (left) celebrates a rare strike against Leyton Orient with Rob Murray (centre) and Cotterill

again with Harry Redknapp at West Ham. Pulis also gambled on Portsmouth midfielder Warren Aspinall. The last time the two men had met was on the field when the Pompey man was stretchered off. A six-game unbeaten run steered Cherries into early promotion contention. The fans sang 'Going up' and the sun was shining, until the Coca-Cola Cup clash with Blackburn when more than 10,000 fans endured torrential rain and a goal-less draw. Beardsmore and Pulis's friend O'Connor were keeping the popular Wood out of the team. The manager was defiant: 'I will pick the team I want, not what the crowd wants.'

ABOVE: Keith Rowland (right) gives Portsmouth's rising star Darren Anderton the runaround

Chief executive Annie Bassett, the reigning Dorset Businesswoman of the Year, was sacked without explanation even though the club was on course to announce an operating profit for the first time in seven years. She said, 'I don't think the board ever fully accepted me because I am a woman.' Jimmy Quinn, the country's leading marksman at Reading, told the Echo his face too hadn't fitted with the new regime at Dean Court. Matty Holmes had a similar story to tell. Pulis, upset by the Bassett, Holmes and Quinn reports, banned the players from speaking to Echo reporter Derek McGregor. Editor Gareth Weekes stuck up for the journalist, calling McGregor a man of integrity and the ban 'an insult to thousands of supporters.' Pulis hit back by claiming that McGregor's friendship with Paul Wood had caused problems in the dressing-room. 'I will not allow an outsider to disrupt and interfere with the operation of the club,' he said in a letter printed in full on the back page of the paper. As sports editor I wrote, 'The manager can't tell us what stories to report or how to write them any more than we can pick his team or decide his tactics.' The siege-like mentality at the club created a sour atmosphere, not helped by crowd trouble at the FA Cup games against Brighton and Nuneaton which prompted the removal of the fencing at the away supporters' end.

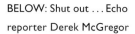

BELOW: Shut out ... Echo reporter Derek McGregor

Just before Christmas 1993 Pulis and Hayward issued a joint statement warning that the liquidators could be on their way in. The coaching staff hadn't been paid for six weeks and the team travelled to Bradford without spare studs because of an outstanding account with a local sports shop. Finance director Ken Gardiner called it an 'unsolicited panic message' and

ABOVE: High-flier Rob Murray made the Scotland Under 21 side

BELOW: Sean O'Driscoll set the record for most appearances

claimed the rest of the board knew nothing about it. The sale of Masters to Wolves in a £600,000 deal helped ease the pressure and Cherries announced a £142,000 trading profit. A bizarre Boxing Day game saw Brentford win 3-0 at Dean Court, Bartram score an own goal, Denny Mundee on target against his old club and Cotterill miss two penalties. Cotterill apologised to disgruntled supporters as he left the field. It was a disappointing end to a depressing year.

MEMORIES – Tony Pulis guided Gillingham to Wembley in the play-offs after leaving Bournemouth and then went on to manage Bristol City. Speaking to the Echo in January 1997, he said …

'The biggest mistake Bournemouth ever made was forcing Norman Hayward to resign as chairman. The club was bankrupt when he took over. We worked very hard for two years to cut wages, sell the best players and just keep our heads above water. A trading loss of £800,000 was turned into an operating profit. It had to be done, although a lot of the supporters didn't realise that. Norman took a lot of criticism over his directorship and my management and it made him ill. But he knew what he was doing was beneficial to the club.'

In October 1998, before his Gillingham side played at Bournemouth and Pulis was ordered from the dug-out and subsequently banned from the touchline, he said …

'Mel has done a great job in putting together a good footballing side despite all the problems going on around him and the team. Dean Court is very much like Priestfield, an old-fashioned ground. I always look forward to coming back because I spent 10 happy years at the club.'

Sean O'Driscoll almost didn't get the chance to break Ray Bumstead's 462-game appearance record as he was given a free transfer by Harry Redknapp and then recalled following Tony Pulis's appointment. On the brink of his historic achievement in December 1992, he said …

'It will be a nice honour if I get the record but the games coming up are just like any others as far as I'm concerned.' (Pulis revealed, 'I probably argue more with Sean than anyone else, over anything and everything. But I have a tremendous respect for him, both as a player and as a person.')

CHAPTER 17

The Great Escape

Bournemouth came to grief on Preston's plastic pitch and were bounced out of the FA Cup. Not a good start to 1994. Pulis and McGregor, although back on speaking terms, still weren't best buddies. The manager reported that on-loan Warren Aspinall had been told to lose weight. The player said, 'I just laugh when people call me Blobby or Sumo. I've been called a lot worse.' Pulis admitted, 'I have made plenty of mistakes. I accept things could have been done differently. But all along I have made decisions with the football club at heart.' And no one could argue with that.

Christchurch-born Neil Moss, like Jamie Redknapp a former Twynham pupil, made his home debut in place of the injured Vince Bartram and played well to keep the score down to 3-1. Aspinall finally signed from Portsmouth at the end of January for a slimline £20,000 while Kevin Russell joined from Burnley and for a while was a hit with fans who would wear rubber washing-up gloves on their heads and chant, 'Rooster!' (The Russell transfer caused a split between Norman Hayward and other board members over who was putting up the money.) McGorry and Wood were both sold cheaply and just over 3,000 diehards watched the no-score bore against Hartlepool after which Norman Hayward gave Pulis the dreaded vote of confidence. The gate was down to below 2,400 when Cherries picked up their first home win in three months against Cardiff. Parkinson was sold to Everton for a guaranteed £400,000 with another potential £350,000 to come depending on appearances. Cherries got £250,000 immediately but the trend towards 'knock ons' made some supposedly-big-money deals hard to decipher.

The low point was the dismal goalless draw at home to

ABOVE: Local hero Neil Moss

BELOW: Who ate all the pies? Warren 'Sumo' Aspinall faces up to his terrace tormentors

ABOVE: Alex Watson (top) and Mark Morris prepare to tackle beanpole striker Kevin Francis

ABOVE RIGHT: The Rooster has landed . . . Kevin Russell milks the supporters' applause

Rotherham when many in the paltry 3,000 crowd joined in shouts of 'What a load of rubbish.' Beardsmore, upset at being left out of the team, asked for a move. For once there was nothing depending on the final game so Cherries, whose home record had been terrible, beat champions Reading. And Fletcher scored. And there were 7,000 inside the ground. And Moss, who was keeping Bartram out on merit, pulled off a stunning save to deny Jimmy Quinn what would have been his 41st goal of the season.

Ex-boss Dave Webb denied he was about to buy the club. Ted MacDougall, now living in Canada, offered to help. He said he had been shocked during a brief visit to Dean Court about a month before. 'It was like a ghost town, almost as if it had been abandoned,' he said. Norman Hayward, exhausted by his three-year stint as chairman, put the club up for sale and Gardiner headed the takeover bid. Luther Blissett came back to Bournemouth, but only to open a sports shop next to the ground selling the new kit, traditional red and black stripes replacing the old 'Pizza Hut' tablecloth design. The takeover was drawn out but eventually went through. The deal would drive a wedge between Gardiner and Norman Hayward and the feud would resurface almost three years down the line. Pulis was

115

sacked by chairman-in-waiting Gardiner who was keen to lure Harry Redknapp back. In the two years under Pulis Cherries had won 26 and lost 34 out of 92 League games, scoring 96 goals and conceding 111. He had spent less than £400,000 and brought in a potential £2.6m (including additional payments). Gardiner wanted someone who believed in bright, attacking football. But it wasn't easy to get the right man. Redknapp, who had shown loyalty to Bournemouth, was now demonstrating the same virtue at Upton Park and within weeks he had taken over from Bonds as Hammers manager.

So Cherries kicked off the 1994/95 season with the takeover dragging on and a committee of John Williams, Sean O'Driscoll and Mark Morris in charge. The whole situation was shambolic, results were awful but the fans supportive. Ronnie Whelan and Bobby Gould were linked with the manager's job before Colin Lee, Mark McGhee's assistant at Reading turned down a three-year contract. Finally, some weeks into the season,

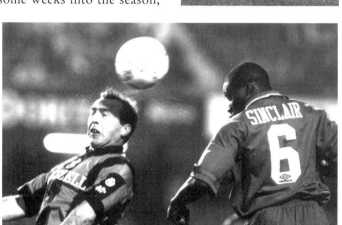

Cherries got their man, former player and ex-Manchester City and Barnsley boss Mel Machin. Cherries lost their opening seven League games, equalling a 39-year-old record, before finally picking up their first point against fellow strugglers Chester, also still to get off the mark before visiting Dean Court. Even at this early stage of the season Bournemouth looked doomed. 'It was getting a bit embarrassing,' admitted a relieved Machin, back in the game after a break of nearly two years. The club was in the middle of another injury crisis, with nine men on the treatment table. Machin made a mental note of their names and, one by one, they left.

The takeover was finally signed and sealed at the end of September, coinciding with the first League win, 3-2 over Cardiff, and Beardsmore's first League goal for the club. New keeper Ian Andrews, in for the shellshocked Moss, played a

ABOVE: Chelsea's Gavin Peacock, back on his old stamping ground, takes on Scott Mean

TOP LEFT: Fiery Jason Brissett (left) explains the rules to Crewe's Martyn Booty

CENTRE LEFT: Chelsea's Frank Sinclair outjumps Aspinall

LEFT: Tony Pulis puts a brave face on things as he walks out for the home game with Rotherham

blinder at Chelsea in the Coca-Cola Cup first leg to put Cherries in with a big chance in the second leg in front of almost 10,000 fans but ex-Bournemouth man Gavin Peacock scored the game's only goal for Glenn Hoddle's side. A 3-0 defeat followed at Shrewsbury whose manager Fred Davies tipped Machin, a former teammate at Bournemouth, to keep them up. Not even the National Lottery's Mystic Meg would have agreed with him. Machin picked up defender Neil Young, strikers Steve Robinson and Steve Jones plus enigmatic winger Jason Brissett. They were to prove inspired signings although Jones was slow to get off the mark and Young's slip on his debut gave Brentford victory. It was the New Year before Bournemouth picked up only their third win of the season, 3-2 against Swansea, to move off the bottom of the table. Fletcher, who had started the campaign in defence, scored twice. The first away win followed at Bradford a week later with Brissett 'unbelievable', according to his manager.

Cherries continued to do pretty well away but kept losing at home. By the end of February fans were beginning to wonder whether their team could achieve the seemingly-impossible and pull off what the Echo was calling 'The Great Escape.' Six thousand fans saw Jones score his first goal at home in a morale-boosting win over Birmingham. Slowly but surely the gap was closing on the teams above. The police, mindful of the Leeds riot five years earlier, ordered Cherries to bring forward their last game of the season. The club, with some justification, were angry, claiming it would hand an unfair advantage to their relegation rivals and pointing out there was quite a difference between Leeds and Shrewsbury.

A crucial battling home win over Leyton Orient was secured with a goal by young substitute Matt Holland, on loan from West Ham, and Cherries drew level with Cambridge United who were clinging on to the last stay-up place by virtue of having scored more goals. Holland signed permanently. A stunning 2-1 win at Brentford in the penultimate game, with goals by

ABOVE: Adrian Pennock on the crest of a wave of adulation following the Great Escape

118

ABOVE: Goalkeeper Ian Andrews shouts for joy as safety is assured

BELOW: Mark Morris

Mean and Jones, lifted Bournemouth out of the doomed bottom five for the first time. A win over Shrewsbury would guarantee safety. A capacity crowd – officially 10,747 but in reality nearer 13,000 – was there for a night of incredible emotion. Brissett unlocked the Shrews' defence to set up the first goal for Robinson after just eight minutes. The tension lifted some more as Mean got the second and Robinson scored again inside the first 20 minutes. The players and fans celebrated at the end as if they'd just won the title. Captain Mark Morris said, 'We kept believing in ourselves and so did the supporters. We were dead and buried at Christmas. It has been a remarkable achievement.' Mission Impossible had become Mission Accomplished.

MEMORIES – Mark Morris returned to Bournemouth after his playing career ended to run a pub in Southbourne ...

'At the start of the Great Escape season we had no manager and barely enough players. Myself, Willo and Sean (O'Driscoll) picked the team and it was quite easy really, we just wrote down the names of 13 fit or nearly-fit players. We didn't win a game, didn't even pick up a point, for ages, not even after Mel joined as manager. But he brought in new players and gradually things turned round. After Christmas we went on a remarkable run and played like promotion contenders. That night against Shrewsbury when we knew we had achieved what no one thought possible, it was absolutely fantastic. It's one of those games that will stick in my mind for as long as I live. Another is the previous game, when we won at Brentford to give ourselves a chance of staying up. We went through a torrid couple of years because of all the financial problems. Wages were often weeks late, which was difficult for a family man like me. It was really dicey for a while, but that made what happened even more special.'

RIGHT: Steve Robinson (left) and Steve Jones savour the moment

CHAPTER 18

Trust in the Future

Mel Machin had provided the perfect riposte to critics who claimed he should have gone for experience over youth and was rewarded with a new three-year contract. And Steve Fletcher had shoved the terrace tormentors' taunts back down their throats to earn the player of the season award. Typically, he modestly said it had been a team effort. The manager continued to rebuild, bringing in young players from Premiership clubs, including Mark Rawlinson from Manchester United, and even spent £40,000 on a comparative veteran with no previous League experience, 26-year-old John Bailey, from Enfield.

BELOW: History-making hat-trick hero, striker Steve Jones

Tony Pulis, meanwhile, was back in work at Gillingham, where he proved to be a big success before departing in acrimonious circumstances for Bristol City, and Harry Redknapp tipped his old club to make the play-offs. Steve Jones became only the fourth player in Cherries' history to score a hat-trick in the opening home game following on from Alfie White (1933), Peter Thompson (1962) and Colin Clarke (1985). He failed to equal the joint record of Jack Cross, Stan Newsham and Ted MacDougall of scoring in six successive games but Cherries still went joint second with a home win over Rotherham. Matt Holland, who got one of the goals, played almost half the game with a broken arm. There were angry scenes as referee Barry Knight sent off Adrian Pennock and Neil Young in the home defeat by Crewe and crowd violence again briefly reared its ugly head as Brighton fans, protesting against the sale of the Goldstone Ground, fought with police during a live televised game. Defender Michael Duberry went down a storm while on loan from Chelsea but Cherries couldn't raise the £150,000 it would have cost to sign him

RIGHT: Local boy Eddie Howe, 18, from Verwood, was man of the match on his home debut

permanently An inconsistent season followed and Ken Gardiner unveiled plans for a new stadium on the present site. Moss kept seven successive clean sheets to equal John Smeulders' record set in 1984 before signing for Southampton for an initial £250,000. There was a hint of the financial crisis to come when a cheque for £9 (a refund to a disgruntled firework display customer) bounced. Youth team skipper Eddie Howe, 18, was star man on his debut in the Boxing Day win over Hull.

BELOW: Matt Holland slots home a penalty against Watford

Total Football magazine claimed Cherries fans were the second-quietest in the country – only Brighton's made less noise. Gardiner appealed for someone to bring a big drum to work up a Brazilian-style samba beat on the South End. But for much of the time there was little for the supporters to shout about. The most remarkable game of the season came at Peterborough. After the previous season's Great Escape this was Escape To Victory. Posh were 3-1 ahead in the 67th minute when Chris Casper, on loan from Manchester United, pulled one back. Three minutes later Scott Mean equalised with his first goal of the season. The home team went 4-3 up 10 minutes from time, Jones made it 4-4 four minutes later and then smashed a sensational winner, the seventh goal of the second half and the sixth inside 21 hectic minutes. Goalkeeper Jimmy Glass, signed on a free from Crystal Palace, was soon picking the ball out of the net five times at Wrexham with Machin reject Kevin Russell scoring twice for the home team. Mean was sold to West Ham on transfer deadline day to stave off an Inland Revenue winding-up order. Ian Cox arrived from Palace on the same day. Cherries finished 14th, Holland was man of the season and Jones, leading scorer with 21, was sold back to West Ham to raise much-needed cash. Dale Gordon joined from the Hammers for a disappointing injury-hit spell as player-coach and Pulis took Pennock to Gillingham.

ABOVE: Eddie Howe (right) was joined at Dean Court by his half-brother Steve Lovell, who later went to Portsmouth for £250,000

Former goalkeeping legend Tommy Godwin, a hero of the 1957 side who made 357 appearances for Cherries over 10 years, died in August 1996, aged 68, and ex-chairman Harold Walker, 81, passed away in October. Supporter Steve Brown was banned from the ground for waving Monopoly money at high-profile Plymouth goalkeeper Bruce Grobbelaar, accused but later cleared of match-fixing during his Liverpool hey-day. It was a

RIGHT: Ken Gardiner enjoys a smoke on the South End

ABOVE: Ian Cox came to Dean Court from Crystal Palace

shame Mr Brown didn't have some real cash to wave around as the financial problems were building rapidly.

Gardiner, a flamboyant figure who would leave the directors' box in the non-smoking Main Stand for a stroll on the South End and a puff on his pipe, promised building of a different kind would soon be starting - he said he would personally begin demolition work for a new stadium to be built, starting in the New Year. But there were rumblings of discontent from inside Town Hall where some civic leaders doubted whether the club had the clout, or the cash, to finish the rebuilding job. Gardiner resigned in early December immediately after returning from a holiday in Africa. His predecessor Norman Hayward, despite not relinquishing his position on the board, hadn't been seen at Dean Court since the acrimonious takeover two and a half years before. But he was back with a vengeance – and a team of financial trouble-shooters including a former

LEFT: Mel Bush watches from his seat in the Main Stand

Portsmouth player over from Australia, Roy Pack. Hayward and Gardiner, both major shareholders, clashed angrily. Hayward had over £1 million invested in the club and he wanted to protect it. Meanwhile the players weren't being paid and the accountants were poring over the books. The remaining directors announced they were 'actively seeking' new investors. Acting chairman Brian Willis said the situation was as bad as he had ever known. 'We have been in a similar position over the past seven or eight years,' he said. 'And something has always come along to keep the club going. But this is the worst scenario in my experience.' The crisis deepened over Christmas when most of the board resigned, leaving just Willis and Norman Hayward in control. Pack was drafted in and when Lloyds Bank called in receivers in January he said, 'This is an absolute disaster.' The players' wages were overdue but they decided to go ahead with the game at Bristol City. It looked as though it could be the last. Steve Robinson scored the only goal as Cherries won against all odds and there followed a protracted struggle to save AFC Bournemouth with Hayward and Pack striving to have the receivers kicked out and a trust led by a group of six supporters seeking to raise enough money to set up a ground-breaking community club based on the Green Bay Packers American football set-up. Pop promoter Mel Bush, a long-time fan, was also in contact with the receivers. Although his campaign was low-key he was deadly serious in wanting to

BELOW: Receiver Alan Lewis on stage at the Winter Gardens

ABOVE: Ken Dando ... one of the trust's leading lights

BELOW: Fans gather expectantly inside the Winter Gardens

buy the club, free of debt, and build a new stadium for use seven days a week, 52 weeks a year. Alliances were formed and disintegrated within days. At times it looked as though the trust may team up with the Hayward camp but Bush always insisted he wanted to go it alone.

The only hope seemed to be a 'white knight', an individual with plenty of money to throw at the problem and it soon became clear that Hayward and Pack would struggle to have receiver Alan Lewis removed. Captain Holland was pictured on the front of the Echo holding a begging bowl the day before the turning point of the whole sorry saga - a public meeting at the Winter Gardens. Behind the scenes, the key men were concerned that not enough people would turn up. They needn't have worried. Supporters were queuing round the block over an hour before the doors opened and once the meeting was underway it was standing room only inside the theatre with well over 2,000 fans crammed in. Trevor Watkins, a young London-based solicitor, held centre stage, appealing for the fans to get behind the club physically and financially. He spoke of his dream - not just survival, but Premiership football. Mel Machin

ABOVE: Mel Machin (left) and captain Matt Holland listen as receiver Alan Lewis breaks the news of the club's reprieve

was visibly moved by the scale of support. 'You wonderful, wonderful people,' he said, tears in his eyes and a crack in his voice. His assistant John Williams, showing not a trace of bitterness despite having just been sacked as part of a brutal economy drive, received three standing ovations. Holland conquered his nerves to take the microphone. It was an evangelical rally, football as religion.

Towards the end of the meeting, a slight grey-haired figure shuffled on stage to a muted, mixed reception. It was receiver Alan Lewis, the man sent in by accountants Arthur Andersen, acting under Lloyds Bank's orders, to sort out the £5 million debt that was threatening to destroy AFC Bournemouth. No one knew whether to see him as hero or villain. Soon there would be no doubt. It was a cliffhanger worthy of Agatha Christie. Lewis, in his usual understated way, told the supporters he had been in talks with the Football League. He had won Cherries a stay of execution. The club would play on, at least for a few games. That was the boost everyone was looking for. Track-suited youth team players walked among the congregation with buckets. Over £30,000 was collected that night and stashed in the New Forest in one of the trust member's cars until it could be safely deposited at the bank the following day. Plans were set in motion for fund-raising events, everything from sponsored silences to rock concerts. Older fans gave up their pensions, younger ones sacrificed their pocket money. This was people power in full flow. The trust fund headed by Watkins and staunch supporter Ken Dando was set up to be independent of the old directors and the receivers and was intended as the conduit for emergency funds to keep the club ticking over until the white knight came riding into town. But as time went on, and the winding-up orders kept coming, it became obvious that the force was with Watkins and Dando and the rest. The trust gradually became more confident and ambitious. The aim now was not just to bail out the football club, but to buy it.

MEMORIES – Trevor Watkins, who became chairman following the trust takeover, looks back on the meeting at the Winter Gardens . . .
'We did not know how many people would turn up. With home crowds of 3,000 and barely 36 hours' notice we weren't sure what would happen. The Football League were debating our fate at the same time that the meeting was taking place – if word came back that we were out the whole thing would have turned into a wake. The meeting was due to start at 7.30pm. Just after 5 o'clock I poked my head out of the door and saw people already queuing up. An hour or so later a tidal wave of people flooded into the hall, packing it within minutes. The supporters took charge of the club's destiny. It was our town, our team.'

Matt Holland left AFC Bournemouth for Ipswich for £800,000 . . .
'The most embarrassing moment in my career so far came a few minutes into my debut against Huddersfield when my shorts split and I had to change them on the pitch in front of a few thousand spectators. I will be eternally grateful to Mel Machin for giving me the chance to play in the Football League and then making me captain. Dean Court was such a friendly place, everyone made me feel really welcome from the minute I arrived, and the fans were just great. I was aware of how serious the financial situation really was because I sat in on a few of the meetings with the receiver. We didn't know if we would soon be out of work but we had a meeting before the Bristol City game and decided to go ahead. Then to go and win there was fantastic. It showed just what's possible when everyone pulls together.'

CHAPTER 19

Up Wembley Way

The trust pulled off a major public relations coup by agreeing to pay John Williams' wages. The hugely-popular 'Willo' was immediately reinstated as Machin's assistant. Receiver Alan Lewis turned down the trust's first offer to buy the club while Mel Bush claimed he had a bid, believed to be in the region of £600,000, accepted and then rejected. The trust, spearheaded by an increasingly high-profile Trevor Watkins, continued lobbying local businessmen for support and eventually raised enough money to satisfy the receiver and his employers at the bank. The next task was to satisfy the Football League who were keen to see the creditors appeased. Another meeting at the Winter Gardens, this time sparsely populated with a few people owed money by the club, eventually saw a CVA (company voluntary agreement) go through. The Inland Revenue would have to be paid off in full while ordinary creditors, including dozens of local businesses, would have to settle for 10 pence in the pound over several years. Ken Gardiner's support (or lack of opposition) was crucial to the CVA going ahead. Norman Hayward, who thought he had agreed a deal with the trust for repayment of his loan and guarantee, was fuming when it was overturned at the meeting.

The League was now prepared to give the go-ahead to a new company, and what claimed to be Europe's first community football club was born. (So far no one else has come forward to say they had the idea first). Cherries, who had seemed doomed to fold at Christmas, scraped through to finish the season in mid-table and looked forward to the next campaign with some confidence. The fans could even look back on a cameo appearance by the legendary Ted MacDougall who appeared as a 50-year-

BELOW: John Williams back in the dug-out . . . thanks to the fans

ABOVE: John Bailey lets rip following the win over Walsall

old substitute in a fund-raising friendly against Southampton. One of the trust's first acts was to increase ticket prices for the new season. Watkins said, 'I am sure the majority of supporters would rather pay more than not have a team at all.' Machin turned down the chance to manage Blackpool then was left distraught by the sale of skipper Matt Holland to Ipswich for a record £800,000. An attempt to lure former striker Jimmy Quinn, 38, back from Peterborough ended in failure while volunteers saved money by giving the increasingly decrepit Dean Court a much-needed lick of paint – a new stadium to comply with the Taylor Report had to be a top priority for the new board. But the 1997/98 season was one to remember because AFC Bournemouth, after 98 years of trying, finally made it to the most famous football ground in the world.

Cherries, especially at home, were becoming a more consistent Division Two force. Although there was the occasional slip-up at struggling clubs they remained capable of playing supposedly better teams off the park and looked a good bet for a play-off place for most of the campaign after getting away to a flying start. Machin had got his young side playing the

129

ABOVE: Mel Machin takes a bow as AFC Bournemouth, after 98 years of trying, finally clinch a Wembley appearance

LEFT: Local lad Christer Warren, on target here against Burnley

ball on the floor with Steve Fletcher offering an important out-let up front and Jamie Vincent dangerous from free-kicks and corners, although the defence couldn't always cope with more direct teams like Tony Pulis's Gillingham. Goalkeeper Jimmy Glass could be infuriating – either brilliant, as when he single-

ABOVE: Stripped for action . . . (l to r) Mark Rawlinson, Jamie Vincent, Neil Young, Steve Fletcher, Franck Rolling, Steve Robinson and Michael Dean

handedly defied Bristol City in the televised FA Cup win over Bristol City, or alarmingly erratic.

But this was a season that would be forever associated with the Auto Windscreens Shield. This competition was formerly the Associate Members Cup (with Cherries the first winners, in the only final not played at Wembley), the Freight Rover Trophy, Leyland DAF Cup and Autoglass Trophy. The Shield may not have been the most revered trophy in domestic football but it was physically the biggest – and offered the only realistic chance of reaching Wembley for most lower division clubs, (although Division Two rivals Chesterfield had come mighty close in their FA Cup semi-final against Middlesbrough the previous season.) Cherries got a bye in the first round and beat Leyton Orient 2-0 in round two with goals by Fletcher and Steve Robinson. Crucially, they were drawn at home for the next two games, which both finished 1-0, against Bristol City and Luton respectively. Vincent was on target against City while French defender Franck Rolling was the hero against the Hatters. Big Franck, a talented chef, was cooking again in the Southern Area final, scoring in the first leg at Walsall with the other goal

LEFT: Miss Great Britain Leilani Dowding gets a lift from (l to r) Jason Brissett, Steve Robinson, John O'Neill, Steve Fletcher, Ian Cox and John Bailey

in a 2-0 win coming from Russell Beardsmore, back after injury to bury a volley from the edge of the penalty box. The Saddlers pushed Cherries all the way in the return in front of nearly 9,000 fans. It was a night to remember at Dean Court, even though the home team lost.

It was a hard but never dirty game yet referee Rob Harris booked 10 players, including eight from Walsall and even the mild-mannered Beardsmore. Harris also ruled out on-loan Mark Stein's effort in a goalless first half with Bournemouth seemingly coasting to the final. But the tie was turned on its head soon after the restart with Wayne Thomas and Roger Boli drawing the visitors level on aggregate. Within two minutes of Boli's clinical finish Cherries were gifted a goal by Walsall defender Wayne Evans when he deflected Neil Young's harm-less-looking cross past his own goalkeeper. Then, with 10 min-

RIGHT: John Bailey steps out beneath the Twin Towers

RIGHT: Directors Andrew Kaye (left) and Trevor Watkins soak up the atmosphere on the big day

LEFT: Jimmy Glass at Wembley

utes remaining, Walsall were on a roll and seemingly on their way to Wembley when another Frenchman, substitute Didier Tholot, scored with his first touch of the ball. Again Cherries hit back within two minutes and again Rolling was the hero, scoring his eighth goal in an injury-hit but eventful season. Fletcher helped the defence to survive five minutes of tension-laden added time and the final whistle and a 4-3 aggregate win triggered scenes of celebration to rival even the Great Escape. John Bailey, the little man who had been absolutely massive throughout the game, tore off his shirt to lead the knees-up. 'When we went two down I really thought that was it,' said Bailey. 'Then I thought of all the people I would have to tell if we didn't make it – and I got stuck in again.'

The prospect of appearing at Wembley took the edge off Bournemouth in the League. The players warmed up for their big day by doing a 'Full Monty' in a plea for sponsored suits and even cut the traditional record, their own unique version of the Bee Gees' Staying Alive with Fletcher on lead vocals. Bournemouth's Miss Great Britain Leilani Dowding brought a smile to the players' faces with a glamorous photo opportunity. Six thousand tickets were sold on the first day and Bournemouth eventually took an estimated 34,000 fans to north London. There was the usual trouble with touts, drawing an angry reaction from Watkins who dubbed this 'The Fans' Final.' And so it was. Dozens of coaches bedecked with banners and scarves travelled up the M3 while hordes of supporters, young and old, made their way by car and train. Ron Hands, president

133

LEFT: Hands up if you love
Bournemouth!

of the Supporters Club, cut short a holiday in Australia to be
at Wembley where three generations of supporters – director
Andrew Kaye, father Sam and son Mitchell – were represented in the Royal Box. Rolling, the man whose goals had been so
important in getting the club so far, was unlucky not to make
the starting line-up against Grimsby. Bailey, who had been selling tickets at the club shop right up until the coach left for the
team hotel, became the first Bournemouth player to score at
Wembley 30 minutes into the game and 1-0 it stayed until half-

ABOVE: John Bailey receives Steve
Robinson's congratulations

time. But the Mariners, also making their first visit to the famous
stadium (they would return at the end of the season to win
promotion in the play-off final) fought back strongly in the
second half. There was an element of luck about their equaliser, scored by substitute Kingsley Black, but they deserved it.
Glass could perhaps have been faulted for the goal but it was
his outstanding save from John McDermott in the dying seconds that sent the game into extra-time.

The first team to score would lift the Shield. Bournemouth
looked the more likely winners then, with a penalty shoot-out
looming, conceded an unnecessary corner from which Wayne
Burnett scored, sticking out a hopeful left boot to send the ball
soaring past Glass. As Burnett, closely followed by his teammates, sprinted off to salute the Grimsby fans, an eerie silence

135

LEFT: Jimmy Glass watches in despair as Grimsby's equaliser goes into the Bournemouth net

LEFT: It could have been me … Mel Machin applauds the Grimsby players as they collect the trophy

descended on the red-and-black half of Wembley. The players sank to the manicured turf in despair, Glass lay prone and goalscorer Bailey sat alone and distraught. The players and the magnificent supporters had given it their all, but it wasn't enough. Cherries may have lost but their performances, not just at Wembley but throughout the season, had won them plenty of admirers within the game. And Richard Usher, marketing manager of Auto Windscreens, praised the 62,432 supporters, including many families with young children, who made up the third-biggest attendance in the history of the competition. 'This was not just passion, colour and sheer noise,' he said. 'There was a warmth and respect for the opposition that was a tribute to British soccer. For the excitement you gave us and the pride we feel in your achievement, we simply want to say . . . thank you Bournemouth.'

MEMORIES – Mel Machin compared his side of the late 1990s with the one he played for under John Bond in the early 1970s. Speaking in 1998, he said . . .

'Over the years Bournemouth have always been recognised as a good footballing side. But I think we are better now than we were when I was playing. Under John Bond people were always saying how the standard of football we played was good enough for the First Division. Our supporters turned up in their thousands because they appreciated the type of football we played. We used to get fantastic support which really spurred us on. I realise the game has changed a great deal since then but I honestly believe that the standard of our play is higher now. Our creativity and movement off the ball and the way the players support each other and keep possession are a joy to watch and far surpass the way we played in my day.'

BELOW: John Bailey

John Bailey reflects on his Wembley goal celebration, and how he nearly blew his big chance of playing professional football at Bournemouth . . .
'After I scored against Grimsby I ran over to the crowd and did a little dance – I didn't realise I was in front of their fans! I was enjoying myself so much it all went quiet in my head. When I was playing semi-pro for Enfield Mel Machin rang me up and asked if I was interested in signing for him. I thought it was one of the other lads winding me up. In the end the gaffer gave me his number and told me to ring him back, then I realised it was straight up. Before that I'd worked on building sites, been a plumber's mate, all sorts. I knew what it was like to work 12 hours a day, real hard physical labour, so I wasn't about to turn down the chance to play football for a living.'

CHAPTER 20

Ton Up Boys

Attendances at Dean Court increased by almost 50 per cent during the 1998/99 season, partly because of the new-found fans who had enjoyed their day out at Wembley, partly because the community club still generated a real feelgood factor and partly because of the presence in the Second Division of big clubs with big followings, notably Manchester City and Fulham, managed by the charismatic Kevin Keegan. It was a season when Cherries continued to make progress, as they had done, on the field at least, ever since Mel Machin's return as manag-

RIGHT: Jamie Vincent's sale seriously affected Cherries' promotion hopes

BELOW RIGHT: Roger Boli had a frustrating time at Dean Court

BELOW: Mark Stein gives scorer Eddie Howe a hug at Barnsley

er. Many fans doubted his judgment, though, when he signed Mark Stein from Chelsea because the diminutive striker had looked short of fitness and out of sorts in his loan spell the previous season, culminating in a disappointing display at Wembley. But the manager was soon vindicated. Stein couldn't stop scoring and with 20 goals by the turn of the year was even threatening to challenge MacDougall's record for the most goals in a season. Big Frenchman Mohamed Berthe was briefly a folk hero before being unceremoniously hauled off in a tough FA Cup tie at Basingstoke. He went AWOL for a while and was eventually offloaded to Hibernian. His fellow countryman Roger Boli, a thorn in Cherries' flesh the previous season at

139

Walsall, proved to be an expensive liability – he struggled with injury and first team sightings were as rare as Lord Lucan astride Shergar. Highly-promising Portugese striker Dani Rodrigues was poached by Premiership neighbours Southampton in an embarrassing transfer mix-up and the lack of cover up front was ultimately to prove extremely costly as Steino's seemingly endless flow of goals suddenly dried up.

Cherries were among the front-runners practically all the way through the campaign. Buoyed by their apparent invincibility at Fortress Dean Court they looked odds-on to make the promotion play-offs for the first time and even cherished hopes of automatic promotion via a top two place. They acquitted themselves well against the bigger sides but continued to lose at places where they really should have done better. Steve Robinson played his way into the Northern Ireland team, Eddie Howe made his debut for England Under 21s while his central defensive partner Ian Cox was regularly watched by a posse of scouts (Bournemouth even felt they could afford to stall on a £1 million bid from Craven Cottage, withdrawn after a heavy defeat at Chesterfield.)

The Football League invited fans to pick their club's all-time greatest player – MacDougall was the clear winner among the Dean Court faithful, although Blissett, Norris and even Jimmy

TOP: Neil Young bursts through

ABOVE: Richard Hughes ... a bargain buy from Arsenal

RIGHT: Kevin Keegan chats with
Cherries chaplain Michael Lowe

Blair picked up votes. Memories of 42 years earlier were revived
with an impressive Worthington (formerly League, Milk, Coca-
Cola, Littlewoods etc) Cup win at Wolves, thanks to the preda-
tory instincts of Stein and an impressive goalkeeping display by
Mark Ovendale. A war of words broke out between Machin and
predecessor Tony Pulis after a dramatic 3-3 draw against
Gillingham at Dean Court. Pulis accused Cherries' players of
diving, Machin countered by saying, 'Now I can see why people here don't like him.' There was another 3-3 thriller at
Reading's majestic new Madjeski Stadium with Bournemouth
fans, packed into one end of the ground, ecstatic as Stein
equalised with nearly the last kick of the match. Machin's old
club Barnsley dumped Bournemouth out of both the
Worthington and FA Cups. Howe was the sole scorer in the 1-
0 home win over West Bromwich, a reprise of their famous
1955 meeting, that saw Cherries through to the fourth round
of the FA Cup for the first time in seven years. Meanwhile,
back in the Auto Windscreens Shield, Cherries chalked up their
eighth consecutive victory, their 5-1 win over Peterborough
beating the previous best run, set in 1970. Almost predictably,
the glittering run was ended by Second Division whipping
boys Lincoln City in the very next game. Still, the government's Football Task Force singled out the community club

141

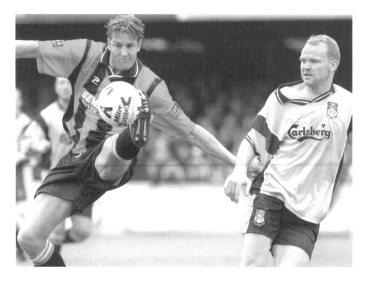

for special praise with chairman David Mellor saying, 'AFC Bournemouth is a heartening example of how clubs in crisis can emerge from adversity invested with a new sense of purpose and stronger bonds with the local community.' It seemed a shame that Mellor, a high-flying Conservative MP until a Sunday tabloid-inspired sex scandal, hadn't mustered as much enthusiasm for his local team during his school days in Swanage.

There was to be no return to Wembley, with Millwall reaching the Auto Windscreens final at Bournemouth's expense, and a hugely-disappointing goalless draw against Wrexham in the final game of the season allowed Wigan to nip in for sixth spot and the crucial final play-off position. A season that had promised so much ended in anti-climax and, despite chairman Watkins' protestations, the sale of Jamie Vincent to Huddersfield on transfer deadline day proved a major blow during an increasingly tense run-in. Vincent's sale brought in desperately-needed revenue – the club were, after all, still £1.7 million in debt – but he had been a key creator of goals, especially from set-pieces. As the club prepared to celebrate their centenary, Watkins issued his book, 'Cherries in the Red, How One Football Fan Saved His Club and Became Chairman', upsetting some fans who felt the title didn't reflect their contribution to the successful resolution of the financial crisis which had almost sent the club spiralling into extinction. Further hefty ticket price increases didn't help the general mood and home gates were down as Cherries

ABOVE: Disappointment after the Wrexham game ended goalless

ABOVE LEFT: Steve Fletcher (left) brings the ball down

RIGHT: A determined Mark Stein

BELOW: Goalie Mark Ovendale

entered the new season and the new millennium. The directors, by now realising that it wasn't easy running a football
club, especially one that called itself a community club, did a
swift U-turn and cut prices in an attempt to lure back the missing fans. Harry Redknapp, in his first competitive match against
his former club, masterminded West Ham's Worthington
(League etc) Cup win at Upton Park. But Bournemouth still had
a football club and the town, a thriving metropolis with major
banks employing thousands of local people and nightclubbers
flocking from all over the country to sample the electrifying
nightlife, could be proud of the way it had pulled together to
drag the team back from the brink. Supporters had a future to
look forward to, with plans for a new all-seater stadium at
Dean Court, the club's spiritual home, gathering pace. And
they had their memories to look back on – three promotions and

ABOVE: Steve Fletcher and Eddie Howe trudge dejectedly from the pitch after the Wrexham game

three relegations, the days of Eyre and Blair, Bond and Supermac, Bishop and Blissett, reaching the second flight for the first time under Redknapp, the Great Escape under Machin. And Wembley, of course, where the bulldozers would shortly be moving in to demolish the world-famous Twin Towers. Yes, even Bournemouth, little Bournemouth, could say they had their day in the sun at the home of football.

The mega-clubs with their millions and their megastores – Manchester United, Arsenal and the rest – were starting to pull away from the rest, even in the anointed Premiership. As Chelsea sent out a team to face AC Milan in the European Cup with a solitary English player, Dennis Wise, in their starting line-up, Cherries were still offering a stage for home-produced players the fans could identify with – players like Eddie Howe, experienced beyond his tender years, the much-improved Neil Young, feisty John Bailey, solid Mark Ovendale, classy Ian Cox, wholehearted Steve Fletcher, tricky little Steve Robinson, the gifted languid Richard Hughes. A century on from the days when the team was picked under streetlamps because times were hard, money was still tight. While the Dean Court directors were striving desperately to raise £10 million for a new ground the all-powerful TV companies were pouring millions into the already-bloated coffers at Old Trafford, Highbury and Stamford Bridge and foreign stars like Bergkamp, Zola and Juninho were topping up their pensions. But AFC Bournemouth were still going, still unpredictable, hammering Colchester then getting stuffed at Scunthorpe, still playing the ball on the ground. The turnstiles were still clicking, the South End still singing 'Boscombe, Back Of The Net!'. Machin, a star player under Bond, was still waving his incongruous baseball cap at the fans, the giant figure of John Williams, a rock for Redknapp, beside him. New century, new millennium. Play on . . . dream on.

THE END (of the beginning)

AFC Bournemouth Fact File

Compiled by Mick Cunningham

FORMED: 1899

PREVIOUS NAMES:

Boscombe FC (1899-1923)

Bournemouth & Boscombe Athletic (1923-1972)

HONOURS:

1946	Division Three (South) Cup Winners (beat Walsall 1-0)
1984	Associate members Cup Winners (beat Hull City 2-1)
1987	Division Three Championship Winners

LEAGUE RECORD:

1923-1970	Division Three (record stay for any side in one division)
1970-1971	Division Four
1971-1975	Division Three
1975-1982	Division Four
1982-1987	Division Three
1987-1990	Division Two
1990 - Present	Division Three/Two (current longest serving club in division)

MANAGERS:

1923-25 Harry Kinghorn, 1925-28 Leslie Knighton, 1928-30 Frank Richards, 1930-35 Billy Birrell, 1935-36 Bob Crompton, 1936-39 Charlie Bell, 1939-47 Harry Kinghorn, 1947-50 Harry Lowe, 1950-56 Jack Bruton, 1956-58 Freddie Cox, 1958-61 Don Welsh, 1961-63 Bill McGarry, 1963-65 Reg Flewin, 1965-70 Freddie Cox, 1970-73 John Bond, 1973-75 Trevor Hartley, 1975-78 John Benson, 1978-80 Alec Stock, 1980-82 David Webb, 1982-83 Don Megson, 1983-92 Harry Redknapp, 1992-94 Tony Pulis, 1994 to date Mel Machin.

GROUNDS:
Castlemain Road, Pokesdown (1899-1910), Dean Court (1910 to date)

CAPACITY:
Currently, because of safety regulations, 10,800

RECORD ATTENDANCE:
28,799 v Manchester United, FA Cup 6th Round, March 2 1957

LONGEST SEQUENCE OF LEAGUE WINS:
Seven, from August 22 to September 23 1970

LONGEST SEQUENCE OF LEAGUE DEFEATS:
Seven, from August 13 to September 13 1994

RECORD LEAGUE WIN:
1956-57 v Swindon (won 7-0)
1939-40 v Northampton (won 10-0), expunged from records following outbreak of
World War II

RECORD CUP WIN:
1971-72 v Margate (won 11-0)

RECORD DEFEAT:
1982-83 v Lincoln City (lost 0-9)

MOST LEAGUE APPEARANCES:
Sean O'Driscoll (423, 1984/94)

MOST CAPPED PLAYER:
Gerry Peyton (seven, Republic of Ireland)

RECORD TRANSFER FEE RECEIVED:
£800,000 from Ipswich for Matt Holland in 1997

RECORD TRANSFER FEE PAID:
£210,000 to Gillingham for Gavin Peacock in 1989

Season	Div	P	W	D	L	F	A	Pts	Pos
1923-24	3(S)	42	11	11	20	40	65	33	21st
1924-25	3(S)	42	13	8	21	40	58	34	20th
1925-26	3(S)	42	17	9	16	75	91	43	8th
1926-27	3(S)	42	18	8	16	78	66	44	7th
1927-28	3(S)	42	13	12	17	72	79	38	14th
1928-29	3(S)	42	19	9	14	84	77	47	9th
1929-30	3(S)	42	15	13	14	72	61	43	10th
1930-31	3(S)	42	15	13	14	72	73	43	10th
1931-32	3(S)	42	13	12	17	70	78	38	15th
1932-33	3(S)	42	12	12	18	60	81	36	18th
1933-34	3(S)	42	9	9	24	60	102	27	21st
1934-35	3(S)	42	15	7	20	54	71	37	17th
1935-36	3(S)	42	16	11	15	60	56	43	8th
1936-37	3(S)	42	20	9	13	65	59	49	6th
1937-38	3(S)	42	14	12	16	56	57	40	12th
1938-39	3(S)	42	13	13	16	52	58	39	15th
1946-47	3(S)	42	18	8	16	72	54	44	7th
1947-48	3(S)	42	24	9	9	74	37	57	2nd
1948-49	3(S)	42	22	8	12	69	48	52	3rd
1949-50	3(S)	42	16	10	16	57	56	42	12th
1950-51	3(S)	46	22	7	17	65	57	51	9th
1951-52	3(S)	46	16	10	20	69	75	42	14th
1952-53	3(S)	46	19	9	18	74	69	47	9th
1953-54	3(S)	46	16	8	22	67	70	40	19th
1954-55	3(S)	46	12	18	16	57	65	42	17th
1955-56	3(S)	46	19	10	17	63	51	48	9th
1956-57	3(S)	46	19	14	13	88	62	52	5th
1957-58	3(S)	46	21	9	16	81	74	51	9th
1958-59	3	46	17	12	17	69	69	46	12th
1959-60	3	46	17	13	16	72	72	47	10th
1960-61	3	46	15	10	21	58	76	40	19th
1961-62	3	46	21	17	8	69	45	59	3rd
1962-63	3	46	18	16	12	63	46	52	5th
1963-64	3	46	24	8	14	79	58	56	4th
1964-65	3	46	18	11	17	72	63	47	11th
1965-66	3	46	13	12	21	38	56	38	18th
1966-67	3	46	12	17	17	39	57	41	20th
1967-68	3	46	16	15	15	56	51	47	12th

Season	Div	P	W	D	L	F	A	Pts	Pos
1968-69	3	46	21	9	16	60	45	51	4th
1969-70	3	46	12	15	19	48	71	39	21st
1970-71	4	46	24	12	10	81	46	60	2nd
1971-72	3	46	23	16	7	73	37	62	3rd
1972-73	3	46	17	16	13	66	44	50	7th
1973-74	3	46	16	15	15	54	58	47	11th
1974-75	3	46	13	12	21	44	58	38	21st
1975-76	4	46	20	12	14	57	48	52	6th
1976-77	4	46	15	18	13	55	44	48	13th
1977-78	4	46	14	15	17	41	51	43	17th
1978-79	4	46	14	11	21	47	48	39	18th
1979-80	4	46	13	18	15	52	51	44	11th
1980-81	4	46	16	13	17	47	48	45	13th
1981-82*	4	46	23	19	4	62	30	88	3rd
1982-83	3	46	16	13	17	59	68	61	14th
1983-84	3	46	16	7	23	63	73	55	17th
1984-85	3	46	16	19	11	16	57	46	10th
1985-86	3	46	15	9	22	65	72	54	15th
1986-87	3	46	29	10	7	76	40	97	1st
1987-88	2	44	13	10	21	56	68	49	17th
1988-89	2	46	18	8	20	53	62	62	12th
1989-90	2	46	12	12	22	57	66	48	22nd
1990-91	3	46	19	13	14	58	58	70	9th
1991-92	3	46	20	11	15	52	48	71	8th
1992-93	2#	46	12	17	17	45	52	53	17th
1993-94	2	46	14	15	17	51	59	57	17th
1994-95	2	46	13	11	22	49	69	50	19th
1995-96	2	46	16	10	20	51	70	58	14th
1996-97	2	46	13	15	16	43	45	60	16th
1997-98	2	46	18	12	16	57	52	66	9th
1998-99	2	46	21	13	12	63	41	76	7th

* Three points for a win
# Premier League Introduced

149

FOOTBALL LEAGUE APPEARANCES

1	Sean O'Driscoll	423
2	Ray Bumstead	414
3	Keith Miller	383
4	Tommy Godwin	357
5	Paul Morrell	343
6	Ronnie Eyre	302
7	John Impey	284
8	Dai Woodward	275
9	Laurie Cunningham	273
10	Ken Bird	249
11	Jack Hayward	247
12	David Best	232
13	Steve Fletcher	230
14	David Stocks	220
15	Tony Powell	219
16	Keiron Baker	217
17	Tommy Heffernan	217
18	Cliff Halliwell	214
18	Chris Sulley	206
20	Neil Young	205
21	Gerry Peyton	202
22	Billy Coxon	200
22	Steve Robinson	200
24	Mark Nightingale	199
25	Ted MacDougall	198

FOOTBALL LEAGUE GOALSCORERS

1	Ronnie Eyre	203
2	Ted MacDougall	119
3	Dickie Dowsett	79
4	Stan Newsham	74
5	Jack McGibbon	65
6	Jack Cross	64
7	Joe Riley	57
8	Luther Blissett	56
9	Ray Bumstead	55
10	Ronnie Bolton	48
11	Denis Cheney	47
12	Phil Boyer	46
13	Trevor Morgan	46
14	Steve Fletcher	44
15	Steve Robinson	42
15	Jack Russell	42
17	Denis Coughlin	41
18	John Archer	37
18	Billy Coxon	37
20	Colin Clarke	36
21	Jack McDonald	35
21	Harry Scott	35
21	Alfie White	35
24	Mike Burgess	34
24	Keith East	34